I Won't Apologize
I Did It On Purpose!

Woman to Woman
A Covenant between Me and Thee

By K'Ceva Barnes

I Won't Apologize, I Did It On Purpose!
Woman to Woman: A Covenant Between Me and Thee

Copyright © 2015 by UImpact Publishing
All Rights Reserved

No part of this book may be used, reproduced, uploaded, stored or introduced into a retrieval system, or transmitted in any way or by any means (including electronic, mechanical, recording, or otherwise), without the prior written permission of the publisher, with the exception of brief quotations for written reviews or articles. No copying, uploading, or distribution of this book via the Internet is permissible.

The author, writers, and publisher have made every effort to include accurate information and website addresses in this work at the time of publication, and assume no responsibility for changes, omissions, inaccuracies, or errors that occur before or after publication. The publisher does not endorse or assume responsibility for information, author and writer websites, or third-party websites, or their content.

Library of Congress Control Number: 2015919821
E-book Version: Kindle
ISBN-10: 0692557334
ISBN-13: 978-0692557334

Preface

There are 13 stones (chapters) written in this book that will address the covenant between you and the Lord. The second set of chapters is a conversation "woman to woman" which allows us to analyze any similarities we may have with other women in the bible, because it is important to bridge our social and spiritual behavior so that our life has a positive balance with no regrets The last part of the book is an "inner" view with yourself which looks at the course of your life and allows you to review your spiritual improvement and setbacks.

There may be some grammatical rules violated by the author's choice to make a point since this book is designed and formatted as an informal conversation between sisters to encourage them to fulfill a life pleasing to the Lord and make no apologies for it.

This book was written in the spirit of humility and in the presence of God Almighty. Have a great journey.

About the Author:

Carol Barnes is a wife and a mother of 5. She holds degrees from CTU in Criminal Justice and Psychology. She facilitates workshops and speaks at women events. She has a passion for empowering women everywhere and encourages them in living their life of purpose. She also partners with her husband in helping educate young adults on preserving their family legacy.

Dedication

To God, I give all the glory. You are the One responsible for the beginning and the completion of this book.

I dedicate this book to my husband, and my children, who with love and sacrifice, supported me in making this dream a reality.

Thank you to my mother, siblings and family members for your love and words of encouragement.

A special thank you to Dr. Rodney Dulin, Bro. Willie Tucker and Bro. Timothy Daniels for inspiring me to serve God with a vision of faith. You have taught me the true essence of how to point up to praise Him, point out to promote Him and to point in to pattern Him.

While this book is a testament of the living sacrifices we face each day, I am forever grateful to all who have shaped my life and given me the courage to find my purpose and fulfill it. Thank you to my spiritual sisters for all your constant prayers, support, and the special covenant friendship we share. That's why this book is dedicated to YOU!

Table of Contents

iii Preface

iv Dedication

Stone # 1. What Mean ye by these Stones?

Stone #2. Broke but Not Broken
    Am I Like: A woman known as Hannah?

Stone #3. God Knows Everything, but
    Am I Like: A woman known as Lot's Wife?

Stone #4. Who Cares?
    Am I Like: A woman known as Leah and Rachel?

Stone #5. My Place of Power
    Am I Like: A woman known as Eve?

Stone #6. Raiders of the Lost Woman
    Am I Like: A woman known as Dinah?

Stone #7. The Right Man
    Am I Like: A woman known as Ruth?

Stone #8 Getting Away From My Wife
    Am I Like: A woman known as Moses wife Ziporah?

Stone #9 The Headless Woman
        Am I Like: A woman known as Jezebel?

Stone #10. Safe Deposit Box.
        Am I Like: A woman known as Rahab?

Stone #11. Five Phases of a Woman
        Am I Like: A woman known as Strange?

Stone #12. All the Single Ladies
        Am I Like: A woman Caught in Adultery?

Stone #13. The Hamburger Helper
        Am I Like: A woman known as Delilah?

Stone #14. Thin Line between God and Mate
        Am I Like: A woman known as Sapphira?

Conclusion: An inner view with myself

What Mean Ye by These Stones

Life is a long journey full of mistakes, losses and victories. Each phase becomes a lesson in spiritual growth. It is a sad thing to walk through this life without unfolding the mystery of why you are here. You are a lump of clay in the potter's hand molded into a vessel to hold the blessings of God.

The purpose of our lives must be performed without wavering or apology. Even the Apostle Paul demonstrates this in Romans chapter 1:16 saying, *"I am not ashamed of the gospel of Christ for it is the power of God."* Following my purpose is never popular. It leaves us vulnerable to skeptics who believe only in self-improvement. It is time that we stop wandering about wanting to find something that we were born to do. To get the best out of life I must put away childish fantasies that only bring more confusion to God's directions.

To my sisters, there is no need to apologize for changing directions and laying aside weights that hinder you. God told Abraham to leave his father's house and he would show him a land that would be given to his seed. God had purposed a work in him that he knew not, but he followed without questioning. Purpose is always misunderstood because it seems selfish and without reason. It is an unknown road with only one sign of direction, "Follow Me." Be strong in your purpose and it will serve many today and afar off. If we live without the knowledge, without the wisdom, without the understanding, we will certainly serve "no purpose".

The Lord has given each of us a purpose under heaven and a course to complete in which no excuses are accepted. This means, He did not leave us without the stones to live by or the power to represent His name.

By this time, we should have learned that all is vanity, and that we should set our affection on things that will please Him. Was the path we chose, wrong? Not at all. While on the way to our purpose we will make plenty of mistakes, take wrong directions, and lose our way. If we hold steadfast to our primary intent, which is to finish our course, God himself will post angels with signs to mark our road.

When I was young, a little girl threw a rock at me. The teacher witnessed it and said to her, "You did that on purpose. Apologize to her", but the girl replied, "No". Even though she wanted to hurt me, she didn't see a reason to apologize for her action. I have found that there are some things you do in life that require an apology, but there are others which need no explanation. The leaders in biblical times wanted Jesus to apologize for saying He was the "Son of God" and He never did. Though people may throw rocks, never apologize for trying to turn your life around to please the Lord.

This is not a book of multiple choice questions with the answers in the back. It is a conversation between "woman to woman" that leaves no stone unturned. We will discuss our behaviors as we move further down the road of equality, and the expensive tolls we have paid on this highway. Toll roads are an expensive way around your problems that will always leave you short of your destination. Do we have a responsibility to each other not to sit by and watch our sisters, daughters, or friends commit spiritual suicide? Yes we do. We are to lend a helping hand every step of the way. Sometimes our stones may be too heavy to carry by ourselves, but this is why God allows us to meet messengers who are responsible for shaping our perspective and our way of thinking. Some are very inspirational, some have challenges in their own lives, and some are directly responsible for the path that you and I are on.

I refer to the following chapters as stepping stones to remember, lest I forget from whom my help comes from. These stones are meant to give you a more positive perspective and challenge the negative philosophy we feed our souls every day.

The Lord used stones to teach us the most valuable lessons in life. Stones were used to kill, build, and leave as a memorial for those coming behind us. In the book of Joshua chapter 4, God instructed Joshua to cross the river Jordan and assigned twelve men to take up stones upon their shoulders. These stones were set to prevent a fading memory and pass on the Lord's victory from generation to generation. When the children ask, "What mean ye these stones?" What will you say? Will we leave the highest testimony of a stone which God turned to bread? My sisters, be a living memorial and a personal testimony of how God takes all things and works them together for good.

Each of my stones, to His glory, was turned into bread. They were no longer a burden or a pile of unstable rocks, because Christ is the Chief corner stone who bless me with faith to understand my purpose. Stones are different and our plight may not be the same, but hopefully our destination is. One of my biggest regrets in life would be to leave my daughters here chained to a stone with no hope. I pray that this book will enlighten some to rethink their journey. When we find ourselves lost, we must pray for wisdom and directions. Our spiritual purpose is no longer written on stones, but in God's book of life.

Broke but Not Broken

A life with purpose is filled with days of ups and downs, with seasons that we most likely don't want to repeat. I believe that communion between sisters develops a covenant through prayer and a place where we can break bread together to express our deepest concerns with confidentiality. We have all taken Satan's prescription for life and felt the side-effects soon after we digested it. When we are broken we live life with internal bleeding. We have highly contagious symptoms of sadness, depression, anxiety, behavioral problems and feelings of loneliness. To make ourselves feel better we say and believe that we are victims. That sounds better and it puts the blame on the offender. If you search the Bible for the word victim, you may not find it. Jesus went through and was tempted in all things but He wasn't a victim, He was victorious. I believe that we have often stained our spiritual mind with negative impressions regarding how life is going and the destiny of our future. Like David, Abraham, Job, Sarah, and Rahab, all who are in the *"Hall of Faith"*, we need to ponder on how to live by faith and understand the evidence of things not seen. There are no magic words or phrases that produce a "Shazzam" moment in our lives.

There is one scripture that gives us comfort on days when we fill empty. Paul says in the book of II Corinthians 12:10 *"For when I am weak, then am I made strong."* Believe me this approach is not for the fainthearted. Take into consideration a phrase that we all have used at least once in our life. That phrase is, "I'm broke". I believe that we may even bring that philosophy to worship. It becomes our excuse to short-change or drive off individuals when asked to pay a debt or help one another. I know what you're thinking, that "I don't have enough money for myself." There is no sin in making this statement. Several people in the bible spoke on this subject. The widow that met Elijah in 1 Kings, chapter 17, she only had a handful of meal and a little oil for her last meal. She was so broke that she planned to prepare a meal for both she and her child and die. Peter who met a lame man at the gate called "Beautiful" is another example of a situation such as this. Peter said, *"Silver and gold have I none."* In other words, I'm broke. But he also said, *"Such as I have, I give to thee",* in other words, "I'm no longer broken". My gift of God is better than the alms that you ask for.

I'm "broke" is only determined by what you have available to give. Have you ever felt at one time that you were of no use to anyone? Sometimes as a woman you may feel spiritually and emotionally bankrupted from a previous relationship and you have nothing else to give. David spoke of this in the book of Psalms, Chapter 31:12, he states that *"He was like a broken vessel"* which had been tossed aside from its purpose. There was a time when we all broke down and fell to pieces, but God put our lives back together and placed His gift inside. I may be broke, but I'm no longer broken. I'm not an empty vessel with nothing in it to offer another person.

What are we really saying when we say, "I'm broke"? My sisters, we can never learn about ourselves without learning about God first. It is God himself that will reveal the inner man behind the shell that we present to others. Being what we call "broke" is an ongoing spiritual examination scheduled by God. We often believe and express more faith in money and the power of what it could do rather than what God can provide. If we had some money, we start to believe that our worries and brokenness would cease. If the truth be told, it was the quest for filthy lucre without conscious which disrupts our walk of faith with God. We must re-examine ourselves and give the most earnest heed, less we fall living a life in fantasy. There is a joy in having money, but money can't be my joy. For what happens when it's low, lost or stolen?

Our joy would be a rollercoaster based on the level of our account. No man can serve two masters; you will either love one or hate the other. There are three earthly riches that each of us protect. We will all protect our health, our wealth, and our family. Do you believe that you are prosperous because you posses good health, good wealth, and a good family? God will surely test uncertain riches to see who is first in our life. How will He know? When calamity comes, your actions and speech will witness against you. We all believe that life without these three blessings is not worth living. Job himself suffered an enormous loss of health and family members in one day. The only thing that was left for Job to hang on to was his integrity. God allowed Satan to touch everything in Job's life including his health, but he could not break his integrity. He is broke but his faith is not broken.

Sometimes God strips us of any idol supplement that can relieve our suffering so that we will approach him as an empty vessel. There is a lesson in this story for both men and women and that is we should store up our trust in God before the evil days come to break us like fine china.

When these three riches are taken or begin to fail what will we say? God broke Job and his reply was, *"God gives and God takes away. Blessed be the name of the lord."* His mentality was "naked (broke) I came into this world and (broke) I will leave." Sisters, God strips us and send us back to our humble beginning to prove us. Should we live life broke? To the contrary, go and make as much money as you can, but not at the expense of your soul.

As a single or married woman we need money, maybe even more than our share and God has no problem with that, but when we ask God for any monetary blessings we learn to ask according to His will, not ours. Whenever we go after it aggressively with our own purpose in mind God blows it away. In James 4:3 *God says, "When we ask amiss we received it not."* My question is not what do we want from God, it's what does God want from us. The answer is "ALL." So He measurers back what we measure to Him. (1) We want all His blessings. (2) We want all His favor. (3) We want all our sins forgiven. (4) We want all His goodness and mercy. Then we want to exchange only some of our resources for all of His, because we're broken; "Bad Deal."

God has put His Spirit in us to bring forth fruit for His pleasure. This means that we must reject the unfruitful works of darkness and be a tree that does not apologize for being planted in God's vineyard, because He will one day come seeking that fruit. Remember, God, may break me to make me over, but if God doesn't do anything else for me He has already done enough for a lifetime. The word "broke" is a universal word used by both the world and children of God. It's a word that was never intended for us to take on in describing our relationship with the Lord. The literal meaning of the word broke should be an uncommon thing for the children of God to use because the word sometimes has a lasting effect on our lives that can bring negative results. We are born again to be rich in Jesus. No matter what state Jesus was in, He followed His purpose and gave to us all that He had. No matter what state we might find ourselves in, we must stay the course.

Let's Talk: Woman to Woman

Our broken promises bring about broken dreams, broken dreams bring the broken hearted, and the broken hearted needs a broken remedy. Our broken remedy is the Lord, because He is not slack concerning His promises. Jesus broke His body for us that we might not be broken again.

Has your broken behavior made you a victim or victorious?

_____
_____
_____
_____
_____

Have you allowed others to break you?

_____
_____
_____
_____
_____

What truth has this stone given you?

_____
_____
_____
_____
_____

Am I like a woman known as Hannah?

How many women do you know have admitted that they were depressed at one time or another? When you sit down and analyze it we are a complex being vexed with so many volumes of concerns. We often find ourselves in the black-hole of self worthlessness. This behavior probably comes from comparing our success to a time table of someone else. Do you remember a day of prayer when you earnestly asked the Lord to supply a legitimate need and you never received it? Afterwards, your attention and focus is fixed on how others are blessed and living so wickedly. We may even feel broken at the time, but the Bible tells us in Galatians chapter 6:9, *"not to grow weary in well doing"*. God knows what we need and has scheduled our blessing in a due season. Therefore, we must rejoice in our tribulation and it will give us the patience we need to wait on the Lord.

By clicking our "NOW" button, we believe that it should call up our schedule form and profile, that says build a student education history, make money, find a suitable mate, and have children at a certain age. Remember education, wealth, marriage, and children are not things built overnight and without struggles. You must have wisdom to manage each of them successfully because they may be overlapping gifts. But when God blesses us with these things what are we willing to give back?

Hannah was a woman whose hopes have been shattered by her inability to bear a child. Being able to bear children during this time was the pinnacle of a woman's life. Often times when a woman could not bear a child she was mocked by other women with insensitive comments. Her day was filled with moping and tears became her food for morning and evening. Even her husband ridiculed her for depressive behavior, as to say, "get over it you can't have children." Instead of relying on sedatives, Hannah began to pray to God. When children of God are burden we must remember we were not made to carry them like an animal. Jesus tells us in the book of Matthew chapter 11:28, *"Come unto me, all ye that labour and are heavy laden and I will give you rest."* We must determine the work and battles that are in the hands of the Lord. We all have our fears and shortcomings and often give up on our hopes and dreams, but God's will is not affected by our reasonable timetable.

Although people may mock you because you are not married, you don't have children, or maybe you have not landed your dream job, it is not an indication that God has said "no" to your desires. In Hanna's prayer to God, she vowed to give the child back to Him if He would only bless her with one. This offer moved God to open her womb and bring forth a son who would become a judge to the Israelites. God always honors a promise of giving before you have received anything, but before receiving any spiritual blessing there must be a sacrifice. Before a nail was put into the hand of Jesus God glorified his name in Him and glorified it again. Luke 6:38 tells us to give and it shall be given back to you with more than you expect.

Let's Talk: Woman to Woman

When our hopes and dreams become shattered it is normal to focus on how we fell or whose fault it may have been. When you fall and break there will be big pieces, little pieces, and pieces you may not even detect. Give the broken pieces to God, and trust Him to be faithful. Your broken pieces are the cares that you cast before Him.

What have you prayed for that God has not answered yet? Explain:

What blessings have you given back to God for the purpose of His kingdom? Explain:

God Knows Everything, but...

Our purpose in life is often never fulfilled, because of a three letter word... "But". This word becomes a stumbling block that can invariably leave gaps in finishing our course in life. The Creator is the Lord of my life and rest assure that He is omnipotent and all knowing. God has a will that has a direct contradiction to my will. His thoughts are not my thoughts and His ways are not my ways. The Lord commands us to walk in the light and shine as women in dark places. Following His command is just an examination of the un-tested faith that lies within us. What the Lord has asked of us may cause us to respond with uncertainty. If you listen closely tomorrow, you will hear the word "but" at least a hundred times. It is normally used in our day to day language to contradict something or someone, but all it does is stall our purpose in life.

In the book of Exodus, chapter 3, the Bible displays a conversation between the Lord and His servant Moses. Moses is summoned by God to begin his purpose which included leading the children of Israel out of the land of Egypt. He begins with uncertainty followed by excuses including the word but. It's sad that we use this word a lot in the presence of God. This reaction often prohibits us from fulfilling our life in Him. To please God, we must believe that He is about rewarding those that honestly seek Him with no "buts" about it. Are you strong enough not to follow the advice of those who trust in themselves? Some may even want a partner on the road to misery, but this is a trip you do not want to take.

I often reminisce about sitting with my girlfriends at restaurants around the city. These conversations resembled TV programs with groups of women, sometimes six deep pouring out their hurts, opinions, resentments, and souls regarding their journey in this life. I am in no way condemning lunch with your girlfriends, but only sit down if you're able to stand. You know how it goes, there is always one who thinks she has it all together by her own will and constantly commenting, "I hear what you're saying "but".

Beware my sisters of entertaining conversations that may corrupt your faith in God's word. I purposely began removing myself from non-productive gatherings that serve me lobster but no purpose, and I have no apologies about it. To move toward your purpose, you need words of life not words of strife. If I have no intention in truthfully helping another better their life I need to "but" out. Nothing infuriates God more than us using the word "but" after He has commanded us to do something. We see this in Exodus chapter 3 during the burning bush experience in the second 40 years of Moses life. Moses explanation of the word "but" was attempting to convince God that He was not capable of leading the Israelites out of the land of Egypt.

Sometimes our purpose may lead us to some of the scariest moments in our life. We often re-evaluate God's will according to the social culture that is in existence today. Do you think the Lord should update or tweak His word just to fit in today's female society? Should He change the book because women are writing their own rules? He is the ruler and the maker, the Alpha and the Omega, all things were made by God and by God all things exist, even women.

Purpose is always given to an individual to magnify works of God and redeem another soul. For instance, when God transforms us, we are sent back into society like Moses who was sent back to Egypt to deliver his people who were enslaved under bondage. Your purpose may lead you to a place where others have failed. You may ask yourself do I fear being a woman of God not with faith or praise only, but with works that are in accord with His will for me.

It is essential to know that servants like Moses were regular people at their lowest and not super heroes. God is the only super hero. Whenever you stand in His armor you may stand with a silly weapon of war, such as a staff like Moses, five smooth stones like David, or with the jaw of an ass like Samson. Our battle today is not against flesh and blood but against principalities and spiritual wickedness in high places. Keep in mind sisters you are the soldier and not the weapon. God already knows you feel defenseless, but the battle is not yours to fight because God provides the armor and the weapon of choice. When women are at war we may be tempted to lay down God's weapon and use our own, but you can't fight Satan with his own weapons. It is the virtue of the Lord who makes your enemies bow and turns their wisdom into nonsense.

A woman's virtue may seem like a silly and outdated weapon to fight with against her enemies, but remember after the battle with the Philistines Samson was the only one left standing. Virtue in a woman is wisdom that God uses to confound the wise. When God calls us to walk in His light, you may want to check in your bag of excuses and compromises. It is only normal to be fearful and unsure when we come to crossroads in our life. Finding your purpose in this life may cause you to stand against a Pharaoh. It took some quality time with God for Moses to weed out his fear of going back to a place where his life was once in danger. God's plan is greater than you and I. We are only a partaker of His righteousness to prove that the world's wisdom is foolishness.

God wants to use us to do the impossible, all the while, in Exodus chapter 3 Moses is saying what may possibly happen. *"God you're almighty, **'but'** don't you know that the slavery in Egypt has been going on for 400 years and had no signs of stopping?" "God you are almighty **'but'** don't you know I'm not an eloquent person?" "God you're almighty, **'but'** nobody is going to listen to me, and I will be mocked."* Moses doesn't have any previous battle of deliverance to give him confidence; only God's word. I often find that, even after God has delivered us from our previous trails, we still believe that our present situation can be handled on our own. The wavering of our faith is often influenced by the world's experiences that sound better than God's wisdom.

I have experienced three types of wisdom. The first one is taught by the world and common to women. This wisdom is based on her experience after hard knocks in her life, banging her head against a brick wall and masquerading that this way of choice is so much more rewarding. Her self-crediting testimonies lead many to this dead end path. This is her version of wisdom which she speaks through a scornful spirit of disappointing experiences and displaces God's truth with "keeping it real". She knows that which she sows will not reap eternal good, so pride forces her to give carnal answers to avoid the truth.

The second is based on hypocrisy. We must be careful not to entertain spiritual instructions that are perverted by anyone. The first lie told to a woman involved Satan telling Eve that God is someone not to be trusted. If the woman would eat the fruit that was prohibited she would find the wisdom and knowledge she was seeking. This is a man-made philosophy that the world never got right from the beginning. This has caused people to seek after wisdom through idols and self-made images which the bible calls dead things.

The third is the true and perfect wisdom that comes from God. This wisdom surpasses all knowledge. This wisdom allows you to speak the truth without fear. This spirit is a heritage that is passed on through generations and stands true to this day. A virtuous woman must present herself with a biography which proves that God is faithful. She must offer a breadth of truth against those who do what is right in their own eyes. So I ask you ladies, which wisdom are you willing to trust?

Your choices in wisdom may require you to lose and choose other relationships. In the book of Joshua chapter 24 Joshua makes a choice by saying, *"Choose you this day who you will serve."* It wasn't a popular statement, and it probably put him in the minority, but the truth does not wavier. He went on to say, *"As for me and my house we will serve the Lord."* This statement covered his wife and children and it should be a covering of protection that every woman should desire for her own home. This was a lesson learned then and it still applies today.

Let's Talk: Woman to Woman

God knows everything about me including the number of hairs on my head and those that have fallen out. God will not excuse us from our purpose while here on this earth. Our obedience to God will lead us to our purpose. The world is devoted to proving that life can work following our own mind and ways. But God can do exceedingly and abundantly above all that we ask and think if we would only learn to remove our "but".

Describe the purpose you have been given and the pros and cons you face.

_____
_____
_____
_____
_____
_____
_____

What biblical principle do you struggle with the most and Why?

_____
_____
_____
_____
_____
_____

What truth has this stone given you?

_____
_____
_____
_____
_____
_____
_____

Am I like a woman known as Lot's wife?

Some of the greatest events in the bible involved women with no name. I wondered why God felt there was no spiritual need to give us the name of Lot's wife. Is it because of what she did or didn't do? In the book of Genesis chapter 19, we find Lot's wife in a place where there was no fear of God. I believe that she may have surrendered to the pressure of the ongoing wickedness of Sodom and Gomorrah. Even though the people of Sodom were considered to be wicked, God wanted to find someone of faith by which He could spare the city. Identity is a key element to every individual's life. God sanctioned the names of all His creations to describe its nature and purpose in this world.

The bible doesn't record a wedding date involving Lot and his wife. We don't even know how they met or from whence she came. God does mention her in the book of Luke 17:32 only to say *"remember Lot's wife"*. In the midst of her deliverance she failed to obey three simple words *"don't look back"*. Her former way of life is melting away and she is more concerned about where she came from than where she is going. Whoever she was in life, God is saying don't be like that. As a matter of fact, Lot's whole immediate family is nameless.

I recognized that God made us and knew us before we knew ourselves. What is the first thing that comes to mind when you hear the phrase Lot's wife? If you said a pillar of salt, you would be correct. What would the Lord think if He called your name? Could He brag or boast about you like Job?

When God spoke to Satan he said, *"Have you considered my servant Job? There is none like him in all the earth"*. Your name is meant to be praised, and there should be none like you so wear it well. Sisters, you will engage in several levels of responsibilities that might include being a mother, a wife, or even a business partner. You will need to rely on the reputation of your name to see you through. We learn a lot based on people's names, including the names of individuals in biblical history. Lot's wife has no name so we can only follow her actions. Without a name she is referred to as that woman "who" turned into salt. What follows after that "woman who" is totally up to you. God wants to forewarn us not to make the same mistakes that others have made. An unwanted identity is like a shadow that follows you wherever you go.

When I was young there came a time when I had to create another identity other than my father's daughter. When I married, I wanted to be referred to as more than my husband's wife. Our Lord was Jesus, the son of a carpenter, but there came a time for an identity change. Men no longer looked at Jesus with a Nazareth background, but referred to him as the Son of God. Who do men say that you are? Do they describe you with an identity that needs to be remembered or forgotten? Do you carry a name that is the same at church, at home, and at work? You should honor your name with the highest respect. Every woman should want God to say her name with no doubt that He is the source of her inspiration.

Let's Talk: Woman to Woman

Your first name is the name of identity. Your second name is the name of authority. There are those who may call and try to steal your identity while here on earth. But God will write our names in the book of life if we obey Him and when He calls us the Lord will say our names.

How can Lot's wife attitude hinder your purpose?

_____
_____
_____
_____
_____
_____

What has God delivered you from that you continue to go back to? Explain why:

_____
_____
_____
_____
_____
_____

Who Cares?

Valentine's Day is one of the most celebrated days to show love to that special man or woman in your life. How many times do we use the word love in our everyday conversations? I hear the word every day but "who cares". The word of God encourages our husbands to love their wives with the same affection that Christ has for the church. Love is a fruit of the spirit, but caring is the component that manifests its true meaning. For example, we may say we repent of a sin, but only godly sorrow worketh repentance. So then love has its own component that worketh it to be true.

In today's society, romance sometimes leads to sexual relationships before any thought of marriage. It's not a new behavior. This is something that has been going on since the beginning of time. In the past there were more restraints put in place to control transgressions such as parental laws, laws of personal shame and civil laws. Once these principles were lifted, the satisfaction of sexual urges dominated any personal shame. Remember, irresponsible urges generally have no fore-thought regarding any penalties that follow. Many women are dealing with *"the night I wish I could take back..."* The betrayal of sexual intercourse only brought about a boat load of scared emotions and haunting memories. Your purpose in life does not involve men trying you out like some showroom demo. That's why there is no need to apologize for being a woman who lives with a standard of respect for herself. This is very important to explain to young women entering into the first stage of puberty.

Every woman should be careful and approach her life thoughtfully and cautiously in this day and time. No matter how tough we think we are God has packaged us with a sticker that says, *"Handle with care."* This is a message to the person who is allowed to handle you. You are the whole package; your beauty, your dreams, your hopes, and especially your love, all wrapped inside and marked as fragile. It is your responsibility to protect what you deeply care about. If you don't care, often times no one else will either. The list of those who say they love you will always outnumber those who care. Express your care and love will prove itself in time.

The book of Ephesians chapter 5 tells us that *"men should love their wives as their own bodies."* When a man loves a woman he will nourish and cherish you as he would his own body. When he cares for you he is willing to make sacrifices for your best interest, and build you up in areas where you may feel torn down. Do you really want love from someone who doesn't care about you? It's a dangerous thing to go into a relationship without a care. I have even told myself, don't marry someone who only says, "I love you," because what is it that worketh his love for me? I'll tell you what it is; it's his care for you. Care is a before and after feeling for you. Jesus cares for His bride. In the book of I Peter chapter 5, the bible describes Jesus' love for us by saying, *"cast all your cares upon him for he careth for you"*.

Love has a willing spirit that cares for another. For example, no woman can say she loves and cares for her child and put a newborn child in a trash dumpster. True care will always bring a feeling of empathy. Caring will cause her to prepare what is necessary for the wellbeing of that child even before it is born. God proves this by His love for us before and while we were yet sinners, before we were born again, before we were conceived, He so loved us. True love demands a demonstration of itself and the Lord cared enough to give us the best of heaven to prove His love for us.

I told my daughter don't marry someone that only says he loves you. These are just Empty words! My husband loves yellow cake with chocolate icing, but there are ingredients which makes the cake he loves. For example; a man once told his wife he loved her very much. One day he and his wife got into a heated argument and the man hit his wife in the eye. She was taken to the hospital because the swelling had closed her left eye. The husband later that day bought her some flowers and balloons that said, "I love you." He did not care that she would be in pain, suffer embarrassment, humiliation, be afraid, and have to heal from the beating. When a man truly cares for you he prepares himself to shoulder your burden. I hope this will help women understand the difference between a "suitable mate" and an "uncaring lover". An uncaring lover is someone who spends the night loving you, but a suitable mate spends his life loving you. If he cares about you even when love is no longer there he will wish the best for you and do you no harm. Remember true love from God never fails. He who loves you will suffer long and think no evil, but rejoice in his love for you. Without true love there only remain false feelings.

Let's Talk: Woman to Woman

You are a tender and fragile spirit, only to be put in the hands of a caregiver. Many have learned this lesson the hard way. Everyone says that they love you, but only a few people care.

What does your spouse care the most about you?

_____

_____

_____

_____

_____

_____

Do you accept love without care?

_____
_____
_____
_____
_____
_____
_____

What truth has this stone given you?

_____
_____
_____
_____
_____
_____
_____

Am I like a woman known as Leah and Rachael?

Many of us own an album of photos which display special moments, people, and places with your family. The most special memories in the photo album are the ones you capture of your children growing up. You see the special relationships they have when they are young and innocent. There is peace and no enmity between them. In the book of Genesis chapter 29-30, a man named Laban, a kinsman of Jacob, had two special girls: one named Leah and the other named Rachel. It was the expectation and custom of every young lady to get married, bear children and raise a family. During the patriarchal dispensation, the father controlled the espousal of his virgin daughters.

According to wedding customs in the biblical days, the oldest daughter was to wed first and then the other would follow. Jacob was sent to Laban's house by his mother in hopes of protecting him from the wrath of his brother Esau. While he was there he saw the two daughters and set his eyes upon the youngest daughter named Rachael. The Bible gives a physical description of both sisters. Leah was described as tender-eyed, but Rachel was described as fair to look upon, which means she was beautiful. When siblings are growing up their physical look is very seldom a problem until an outsider makes a distinction between the two.

If you notice today, many sisters are at odds because of acceptance and rejection of men. A man drops one to choose another and the women become instant enemies especially if neither of them has given up on regaining his love. Listen my sisters, sharing the love of a man with another woman never works out because someone will always get the short end of the stick.

Leah and Jacob were at odds when he chooses to bring Rachel into the marriage relationship after Leah was given to him. Her marriage to him did not change the fact that Rachel was his first and only choice. Jacob now becomes a judge in the family beauty contest. Outsiders have always picked the most beautiful, talented, artistic, and athletic from the impartial family to display that one is better or more worthy than the other. Laban came to the defense of his daughter Leah and would not let Jacob disrespect the order of his family. Jacob was tricked and forced to take Leah first or nothing at all. He clearly made his feelings known that he wanted Rachel and did not want Leah. He vowed to work another seven years for another woman while he was married to his wife.

During this time Rachel drew most of his attention and Leah became sloppy seconds. The only thing that brought Leah joy in this awkward relationship was giving birth to his male children to carry his name. Jacob fathered thirteen children from two wives and their two handmaidens named Bilhah and Zilpah who were given to him to keep the birth race going. This created a battlefield of who could bear children for the affection of Jacob. The strife between the two once loving sisters is being played out, not only in front of Jacob, but the children also. This type of action has us glued to our television sets today. We seem to love it when two women are put against one another in a fight after both have slept with one man. The man watches with amusement as they brawl on stage to prove that he loves one more than the other. These events are marketed and manipulated in today's media for entertainment purposes.

It is sad that Leah had to live her life believing that the man she desired didn't care about her. Leah is one of many who are bearing children with good intentions but with bad results. Romance should be settled before children are involved, but things happen. The night after the wedding feast Jacob goes in the tent to lay with his bride. All through the night he is making love to Rachel, but having sex with Leah. When the morning comes she sees it in his eyes and hears it in his voice that she is not the one for him. She learns a lesson that we fail to teach. It is easier for a woman to stop the sun from shining than to make a man love you when he won't let you.

Let's Talk: Woman to Woman

The affection of the man and wife is not based upon how many children they can produce. This caused a rift between Leah and Rachel which only involved each one's handmaiden to pick up the slack. Even though the whole family possessed a dysfunctional living situation, God still fulfilled His purpose. If the man you love doesn't want you "who cares". God still loves you and that's all that matters.

How can Leah or Rachel relationship help you fulfill your purpose?

_____
_____
_____
_____

Have your relationship with a sister ever been torn apart?

_____
_____
_____
_____

My Place of Power

We have all heard the saying that a woman should stay in her place, but if you heard a man say that today you might have to break up a fight. Before we start, let me say our place in power is not only a location, but it's also a vocation that moves about with you. Believe it or not, I had no say in where the Lord placed me. The first man, Adam, was created and placed in a garden that God had put east of Eden. Adam's purpose in the garden was already set and prepared with water and a very fertile ground. This was his place of authority to move about and rule until he sinned against God. Many since then have decided to reject and reposition themselves outside of His order.

Everything that God made has a purpose and a place to glorify His power. For instance, the sun has a place far above the earth for a reason. How would you like the sun to sit on the earth? Instead of preserving life from its place of authority it would destroy all life. An worm is not meant to fly no more than an eagle is meant to live underground. It is not their place of authority. Why did God put me here? He did it for His own pleasure that others might be blessed and gives glory to the Father.

We as women have a beautiful purpose and place given by God almighty and not by man. God has proven to be the source that controls my fad, fashion, style, sex appeal, and inner beauty as a woman. The true meaning of the term beautiful is the highest compliment given to a creation of God. A woman's style and grace is meant to behold in amazement and wonder. There is a purpose for a woman to maintain the beauty of her temple without and within. You live and present yourself by the power of God each and every day and there is no need to apologize. II Timothy 1:7 confirms that *God has not given us the spirit of fear, but of power, and of love, and of a sound mind.* God has put in His power the three things that bear record of me: my mind, my soul, and my body which works together for the good of salvation.

God tells us that greater is He that is in thee than he that is in the world. Our existence is modeled by our mind, body, and soul. God gives us a lifetime to develop all three. The exercising of these gifts is put at risk from years of speed dating and wasting our gifts on unwanted men. We are living in a perilous time and you can easily become the prey caught in Satan's snare. Women in the book of II Timothy chapter 3 were taken advantage of by men who creep from house to house. In his hunting approach my mind becomes his camping ground. He believes he must enter through my thoughts and trust, breaking down the walls of my integrity. I must never let another mind dominate my thinking other than the power that is in Christ Jesus. I know this may sound like a boring life with too many restrictions. A boring woman is like a lamp sitting on a table unplugged from the source of power, no matter where she is placed she will never shine

Within my mind, lies my gift, regulated and administered by the measure of wisdom given by God. Unfortunately, Eve, in the book of Genesis chapter 3 is a perfect example of mind tampering by letting evil communication corrupt God's given instruction. We must not let anyone seduce us with vain and enticing words that exalt us above measure. A woman must prove all things and try the spirit of anyone to see if it is sent of God. Our mind must judge God's faithfulness according to His promise in our place of power. Promises are not always immediate, but are often times afar off, and they are always on God's time.

Is my body my enemy or my friend? My body is the person who wants to be first. It refuses to be subjective to our spirit and the will of God. It can be used for the power of God or the power of Satan. It is in our power to do one or the other. In 1 Corinthians, chapter 6 it describes my body as the temple of God. It is very important that we understand that there were strict instructions on how the temple should be built. It was a beautiful building laced with the best material available, because it was purposed to house the presence of God. We proclaim today the fact that God lives in us, so why would you let someone desecrate your temple? Baby milk in a beer bottle just doesn't look right. The milk may be unspoiled and good for digestion, but it just doesn't look right.

My sisters, your body is property of God and it should never lie in ruins. The cleanliness and upkeep of this body is your responsibility. There is no power in an empty building. A Christian woman must always be attractive, not to glorify herself, but so that men can see God in her. There is nothing wrong with adorning your body. God created you with a body suitable for the appreciation and the desires of a man.

Just read the book, Song of Solomon chapter 1-2, and you'll read about Solomon's admiration of a young lady's body. Evidently Solomon looked upon her to compare her anatomy to this earth's seasonal features. We all know men stop and stare because their first view of attraction is our bodies. But we often learn a hurtful lesson in life from this, and that is, though we can attract him with our bodies we cannot keep him with our body. Trust not in vain beauty for you will do desperate things to preserve it. Ask any model, prostitute, actress, or the Beyonce wannabe's what the cost for vain beauty is these days. You're only going to shake your booty for a while and after those years a new sheriff will be in town.

This madness has caused many to make ridiculous alterations to their body to impress a society who does not care about them. Remember, God took the time to fashion you and create you in His own image. He has given us the power of His Word to develop a beautiful soul to fulfill the love shared with a man. In Ephesians, chapter 5 the Bible informs us not to defraud our mate, because *the husband hath not power over the wife neither does the wife hath power over the husband.* They have both been given the power of intimacy to keep each other pure before the Lord. This is not only referring to the physical intimacy because attraction is brewed through physical appearance before any disrobing begins. Your husband must always be enticed by your style, grace, sex appeal, and chaste behavior. Never let these lie dormant just because you're married with children. He is flesh of my flesh and my body is meant to be a suitable mating sanctuary to avoid sin against God.

In the book of Judges, chapter 14:2-3 we read that Samson solicits his parents help in his quest for a wife. Samson also gives his parents a reason for wanting his wife. He states that she pleases him well. My sisters, your husband should testify not only of the goodness of the Lord, but also the goodness of his bride. These things may be difficult if we do not learn to love ourselves first in mind, body, and soul. Your soul is the most important asset in your life; not your husband, not your children, but your soul. Whatever you give in exchange for it will only be enjoyed for a season.

There are many souls in Satan's pawn shop because we disrespected the gift, and sold it below its value. A woman's duty on earth is to keep God's commandments and not to put her soul at risk or in the hands of the unrighteous. My soul is everlasting to me and a priceless gift which needs my honest attention every day. There is an ongoing battle between your thoughts, lust, fears, self-doubt, pride, and the war of our flesh. Whether in heaven or in earth, our place of power is always with the Lord.

Let's Talk: Woman to Woman

God says that you are royal not spoiled, and there is no need to apologize. Pray and ask God to endow your place with the power to live a purpose and sail through any storm. We are all vessels with a course set to reach the other side. Any ship not traveling the course of your destiny may need to be abandoned. Blessed is the woman whose regrets have not anchored her to the titanic of life.

What is your weakness in your place of power?

_____
_____
_____
_____
_____
_____

Is your place of power prosperous to others?

_____
_____
_____
_____
_____
_____

What truth has this stone given you? Explain:

_____
_____
_____
_____
_____
_____

Am I like a woman known as Eve?

There are several women mentioned in the history of God's divine epistle. We cannot imagine the life of our first couple honed together by God. No other male or female rivals can compare to them. Each was made perfect in their own right. She is the first woman, wife, mother and soul mate to her man. She was fashioned from the rib bone of her donor, Adam. Her name is Eve.

Eve possessed and experienced the first thrill that motivated the stimulus of the man. God created a woman's love as a priceless gift that is an irreplaceable value to a man. Eve was no longer satisfied with her present status. She collaborated with someone outside who she believed had her best interest at heart. She wanted to be equal to God and was stripped of her home in Eden. I find that ironic, because this is the same reason that Satan was kicked out of heaven. My sisters; be not deceived when Satan sends ungodly conversation your way, he wants you to suffer the same fate he is guilty of. You are a triple threat and the devil knows it so don't let him destroy the blessing of being a wife, mother and even a soul mate.

That which God has put inside of us is a transferable blessing for others. It is our duty to cultivate our blessing by His instructions and catalog. The experience between God and Adam's soon to be mate would have been something to behold. When God said, *"let us make man in our own image,"* He made Adam but there wasn't anything existing on earth that needed Adam. When God created Eve, He looked at the purpose of His man to not only worship Him, but to multiply His glory. When this couple was naked before God, there was nothing to hide or to be ashamed of.

I don't know how long Adam was single before God created Eve, but I believe that the first couple experienced days of heaven with long strolls through the garden, sunsets by the river, moonlight walks with no fear, and the best of everything. Satan is after man, but he wants his woman. Satan wants to lead us to a place that God is telling us to flee from. When Adam and Eve decided to eat of the forbidden fruit their eyes were opened and now they could see each other's nakedness. Now Eve has to hide from God that which she is ashamed of. We all live in shame of something and the guilt follows us. There is no sheep clothing, lies, or hiding place that can conceal our shame from God. God is only blinded by the blood of Christ, which can wipe the guilt of sin away. Satan wants us to hide like Eve when God calls. The devil wants us to believe that we are no longer valuable in the sight of God. Even though they both sinned against God his punishment to Adam brought the greatest blessing in God's purpose.

Let's Talk: Woman to Woman

Look at the creation of the woman in this way. God created you as help meet which means Adam was first, but the one who was lacking. Do that which you were commanded to do. Do not allow Satan to convince you otherwise. You may fall from Eden to emptiness, but the fruit of the Spirit can bring you back to life.

Do you despise your birthright as a woman?

_____
_____
_____
_____
_____
_____
_____

What spirit do you model for young women?

Raiders of the Lost Woman

I know this title sounds similar to an epic thriller made in 1981 starring Harrison Ford. This movie portrays a story of lawless men who are trying to steal the famous Ark of the Covenant, which Israel posses during their journey through the wilderness. Each party would go to any length to obtain it even if it meant killing the other interested party. This may be an extreme case of coveting a possession for personal gain. Let me simplify the title. A raider is someone who comes in your life unannounced searching for the spoils and values you have left. He catches you when your guard is down and you need a friend. A raider doesn't come daily; he's a one-night opportunist. Remember that Satan himself is a raider. In the book of John chapter 10:10 the bible says that it is *Satan who cometh to steal, to kill, and to destroy.* God allowed the devil to attack Job through all three acts of evil in one day. He stole his wealth, killed his servants, and destroyed his family, but Job did not sin before God.

During the course of our lives we will come in contact with different forms of raiders. Many women find this to be true after failed relationships. I have often observed women in different places talking on their cell phones screaming at some raider who has made an unlawful entry. Afterwards we might seek the comfort of a female friend to discuss the secret of our broken heart, our feelings of abandonment, and our feeling of loss during this time. We feel abandoned simply because a place in our soul that was once occupied by a person is now empty. Someone left and didn't even leave a message. Someone ordered love and left an insufficient check that bounced. I'll leave you a tip: Jesus will never leave you nor forsake you. The thing I find disturbing is how we solicit advice from every corner of society rather than the chief corner stone.

When I'm lost, I am not only without direction to find my way, but I am in a place waiting to be picked up by anyone. It is for certain that trouble will come our way; it doesn't need our invitation. When you post your bulletin stating, *"I'm lost,"* you automatically RSVP an army of raiders. Your wounds are open and bleeding with the smell of blood. A raider parades under a banner of concern for you, but all the while waiting for the sun to go down. I find it funny that every time there is a social disturbance, looting always follows. Peaceful demonstrations are filled with those concerned about the victim, but it's also filled with raiders using the occasion for their own motives. So when you post on-line that you have been a victim you are empting yourself to the wrong audience, and you are personally inviting raiders to make an unlawful entry into your unguarded dwelling.

Don't turn your trials into fear and desperation because when desperation sets in, your standards leave. There was a time when men were more likely to retreat from their standard age to pursue young prey. Now women are saying we want a young man, single and free, experienced in love preferred, but will except a young trainee. Don't put yourself at risk with a raider who will steal the spoils you have remaining. Raiders will come masked. They are smooth talking; they take without remorse what is not theirs to furnish another relationship. Stand firm my sisters and be not deceived. Raiders are not only men, but there are countless women who poured their secrets into raiding women who stole their man, their children, and their dreams.

Let's Talk: Woman to Woman

Remember a raider is an invader. Be careful what you post about yourself. Beauty is like fly paper. You may set it out to catch one thing and find yourself stuck to all sorts of things you can't shake off.

Has your home ever been raided? If so explain:
_____
_____
_____
_____
_____
_____
_____

Have you ever posted the wrong image on facebook?
_____
_____
_____
_____
_____
_____
_____

What truth has this stone given you? Explain:
_____
_____
_____
_____
_____
_____
_____

Am I like a woman known as Dinah?

Have you ever experienced a time in your life when you felt like you were not important amongst your family? Don't worry, you are not alone. Whatever you go through, you are not the first. There is always someone who has walked the road that you are on. In the book of Genesis, chapter 30, we find that Leah had 6 sons with her husband Jacob. The Lord blessed her one final time with a daughter, and she named her Dinah. It appears that Dinah had to live in the shadows of her 12 brothers, never getting the kind of affection or recognition she felt she deserved. This may have caused her to live in a shell or to leave with the idea that you're missing something in life. This kind of neglect can sometimes cause a woman to seek attention in other ways. Many young ladies will tell you that their problems began when they had set their sights on things outside the comforts of home.

One day Dinah decided to go into town and see the other women in the land. She is young, alone, and no one knows her whereabouts. During her visit she is seen by Shechem, the prince of Hamor. The Bible says that in Genesis, chapter 34, he took her and had sex with her. While he humbled her, there is no violence mentioned in this act, or any mentioning of her resisting. Some say she was taken as a wife and others say it was outright rape. Since she is Leah's youngest child, we may not know her exact age. In this society if she is under age it would be statutory rape, even if she agreed. In biblical days, unless a law or a custom existed, there was no violation. The definition of "humble" is given in the book of Deuteronomy chapter 22, expressing against a man who woos or wears the woman down to finally give in.

Shechem's subtle speech and royal appearance probably lured her to the point of no return. The Bible also says that his soul claved unto her when he finished. Notice that his soul claved and not her soul. He loved the damsel, and spaked kindly to her. No matter what words of comfort is given, the deed is done. Shechem is no amateur, and he most likely believes his royal privileges gave him the right to fulfill whatever his heart desired. Many women have a story about a time they found themselves in an area of restraint with a person who had the wrong expectations.

Un-consensual sex is always one sided and it only benefits the vile pleasure of the offender. Many women live with the secret of rape or unwanted advances from someone they trusted. This fear lingers for a long time. There is no prescription pill to erase this from the frontal lobe bank of memories. She is not only affected but she is also infected. She becomes an inmate in the emotional prison of this violation which only a greater love can begin to heal. We are so conscious of the fear of rape that we carry mace, double lock our doors, and take self-defense classes. What we do above anything is ask the Lord to lead you not into temptation and deliver you from evil. There is no ransom, no gift, no rest or contentment for this crime. Many women have been ushered into this hell hole without a savior.

We must always pray and ask God to put His hedge of protection around us and protect us from this menace to society. Our daughters are in school, neighborhoods, and have jobs with males who have a Shechem mentality. If we keep God's commandment and bind them about our neck, then no man can take me. We don't hear anything else about Dinah after this event.

The book of Proverbs 6:22 says that the law is my guide, where I go it will lead me, when I sleep, it shall guard me, and when I awake, it will talk with me. During those times there was little to no redemption for women who had been defiled. Dinah's brothers eventually came to her rescue and killed her attackers, but who can kill the memory, the pain, and the regret she feels. Is she continuing to walk in the light or living back in the shadows again?

Let's Talk: Woman to Woman

If you have ever experienced this tragedy in your life, you may still be dealing with the brokenness, pain, and blame. Many people may try to analyze how you feel, but only God can fully heal you. For God has an angel among us to comfort the trouble-hearted.

In what areas of your life are you most vulnerable?

_____
_____
_____
_____
_____
_____

If Dinah was your little sister how would you encourage her?

_____
_____
_____
_____
_____
_____

The Right Man

There are so many decisions we make in our lives. These decisions require choices to be made and usually they involve other people, especially men. Do you want to get married someday? Do you want children? How many children do you want to have? Our choices are our own and should be made through logical wisdom and not emotions. One major choice is finding the right man. Who is he? The bible states in the book of Proverbs 31:10, *"Who can find a virtuous woman?"* Maybe, the right man can. He is a positive influence and a motivating force in your life. A woman has many choices and will get her share of proposals, but she hopes that the man who she selects is the right man. What do I need to look for when finding the right man?

Many women will put his physical attributes at the top of the list followed by his wealth and his possessions. A man's physical attributes may be the first thing you see, but it's not the thing you look for. Our physical attraction is not enough to hold onto because young turns to old, good looks are definitely fleeting, laughter may turn into tears, and riches can turn into poverty, and so on. Risky, isn't it? We are all spiritual beings covered with a body of flesh that has no future. If I desire to be joined to a man for the latter and most important years of my life, I have to make the right choice. When God chooses men to rule over his house they all had to meet his qualifications. In I Timothy chapter 3, the bible lists the qualities a man should have if he desired to Shepherd the Lord's house. These men were commanded to feed and watch over the souls of the family of God. The bible outlines these spiritual qualifications so that there will be no mistakes when choosing a man. Women should have a similar list of qualities before a man is ordained as head of the household to avoid any mistakes.

Who is the right man you ask? Well...

(1) He is a man that is righteous. Why do we need a righteous man? Do you want God's blessing and watchful eye on your home? The right man will be a prayer partner when evil times come. In the book of James chapter 5:16, the Bible says that *the prayers of a righteous man availeth much.* The most desirable man today is one who is clothed with the blessings of assurance that God is his deliverer. There is nothing boring about him; his style is his grace and his swagger is his confidence in the Lord. The most desirable man today is one who values the word of God and is passionate about the well-being of his family. You need this man because he shall be blessed by God and while you are with him you will be his beneficiary.

(2) He is an upright man. If I am going to wear another man's name other than my father's, it must mean something. He must walk in integrity. A good name is better than riches. You will deliver off-springs and nurture his heritage, but the integrity of his name will be the heart and soul of his house. A house is not a home built with a single man's philosophy. He stands tall in his house and is a model that many want to imitate.

(3) He is one who knows the right from the left. Ladies do not accept an imposter. In the book of Matthew chapter 25, Jesus describes himself as the shepherd who shall gather all men and separate his sheep on the right side from the goats on the left. A goat is a bull headed animal that follows the beat of his own drum and rambles through life ignoring instructions. The man who knows the Lord's right side will prove himself every day. You don't need a hardheaded man with his conscience seared. Always look for a man who has an open mind that God can speak to. He has no fear in walking upright and wants to stay on God's right side. When everything is going left he has the strength to say, "As for me and my house" which means he is setting the example of government in the home. I can follow that!

(4) I need a right now man. Believe it or not there are a lot of males out there but many of them are entangled with social issues. The right now man refuses to let drugs, incarceration, alcoholism, and domestic encounters destroy his integrity. The hang-ups are sometimes a result of extended adolescence. He won't grow up. I need a man right now, not later, not after a while, but right now. Paul says when you become a man you put away childish things. No woman wants a man who cannot intellectually, mentally, and spiritually keep pace with his family.

(5) I need a man who has the right-a-way. Relationships have many intersections. He is in his car of opinion and I am in mine. Who has the right-a-way? This man has the right to me. I am his and he is mine. We are never to defraud one another or deny any needs to be met. God watches the right-a-way in our relationship. I want my man to have the right-a-way to me. This right-a-way is also a mutual agreement between the two individuals to know one another in order to prevent martial trespasses.

I gave those five examples listed above as a guide for expectation, not an ultimatum. Many women have opened their doors for men who made no preparation to oversee the souls of a family. There have been a growing number of women who have confessed that they were victims of the wrong man being let into their home. Even some celebrities speak of being a child violated by men who were snakes in the grass. In the book of Genesis chapter 3, we find Eve in conversation with the wrong man. Her fault was keeping the company of a pet snake. I'll tell you a story that is tragic but hopefully it will make you conscious the next time you choose a man.

There was a woman who had a pet python she kept in a cage inside her house. She would take the python out every day, feed it and let it curl about her. She also was the mother of a newborn baby girl. One day she took the snake out to feed and pet it. While she was petting the snake the phone rang. It was her girlfriend on the other end. She put the snake back in the cage but forgot to close the door. She talked with her girlfriend for a few hours and finally said goodbye. She walked by the cage and noticed that the door was open and the snake was gone. She began to search the house. She stopped and realized that her child had been asleep for a while in the other room. When she entered the room she looked over into the baby crib and saw that the child had dents and teeth marks on her little body. She screamed hysterically and grabbed her child in disbelief. The snake had smelled the milk from the baby's bottle and made its way to her room. She looked up and saw the pet snake on a shelf above the crib curled up, quiet, and with no conscious or remorse about what had been done. She called the paramedics and the authorities to come and remove the snake, but it was too late; the child was dead. I know this was a graphic story, but we are losing the war on violence in the home. You pick your poison. Will it be your child or your snake?

Let's Talk: Woman to Woman

In your quest for a relationship, don't feed and pet snakes nor let them in your house. The right man has a conscious and doesn't sneak around. He is always conscious minded to protect and ensure that his presence is a comfort of security in his home.

What type of men do you attract and why?

_____
_____
_____
_____
_____

Are you looking for the right man in all the wrong places?

_____
_____
_____
_____
_____

What truth has this stone given you? Explain:

_____
_____
_____
_____
_____

Am I like a woman known as Ruth?

We all suffer tragedies in our lives but who knows how things will play out. Take a good look at the life of Ruth in the book that bears her name. We find in chapter 1 that death has taken the husband of Ruth, Naomi her mother-in-law and Oprah her sister. Each woman has suffered the death of their spouse in a short period of time. Some women may deal with this fact of life differently. You may be a part of the family as long as the husband lives, but when he dies how is your relationship sustained? Does the present life go on or is it back-to-the-drawing board? These two young women are left without any resources or any children to support them. One sister chooses to go to an old familiar life, but Ruth decides to trust in the God of her mother-in- law.

My sisters, be careful and do not choose a man who does not make provision for you through life and after his death. On top of your sorrow you are left to bury and pay debt left behind. The love of the right man will never leave you without financial support. Through our Christian journey we will be faced with the death of a loved one. When you have separate beliefs, live separate lives, you will go separate ways. Ruth and her sister Oprah are Moabites; they worship idol gods and have no personal relationship with the Lord. If your spouse passes away, what are your plans? Do you take the wheel and keep going forward or do you park along the side of the road and wait on another driver?

This is a crisis that will bring us face to face with many decisions. One in particular is: "How do I go forward?" We have had so many relationships with fragments of our love and emotions left in them. There is always a risk when moving into another relationship with thoughts and feelings of uncertainty. Our hearts are filled with many questions. Do I need to take more time? Is this a better man? Will he cause me harm? Be cautious; relationships are not made for testing you as the specimen. Like the science lab, once the experiment is finished the specimen is thrown away.

God took my mate and now what? Unfortunately, many women rush into another relationship without allowing God to heal the hurt that we feel. Relationships are stressful enough without living in fear of the big three: death, divorce, and desertion. These three may subconsciously leave you with a widow mentality. Ruth was faced with this dilemma and made a decision to press forward. She attached herself to the source of strength she witnessed in Naomi who suffered the same loss and held on to her faith in God. There was no need for her to search for the next man because he found her. Negatives in life may cause us to think our purpose is over, but stay prepared no matter what. Ruth didn't know that she was headed to the second half of her life, which would actually be better than the first.

Let's Talk: Woman to Woman

Perfect love can cast away all fears. These are the words to make love by: *"I'll lodge where you lodge, go where thou goest, and your God will be my God."* Life is short and time is wealth, so spend it on your purpose.

What have been your difficulties in or leaving a relationship?

_____

_____

_____

_____

_____

_____
_____
_____

How can the commitment of Ruth help your purpose? Explain:

_____
_____
_____
_____
_____
_____
_____

Getting A-way from My Wife

Have you ever witnessed a couple arguing in public? Sadly, I have. I watched a husband and wife cursing each other at a gathering one day. Both of them were so engaged in their anger toward one another they didn't notice that a crowd had gathered. People had their camera phones out and prime time videos were being posted. I vividly heard an elderly woman in the crowd yell, "That's not the way you talk to your spouse!" The word of God always shows us the way to treat others. Your way should not be a burden, but a gift that spiritually impacts the life of another person.

In Ephesians chapter 5, God instructs husbands to love their wives the way Christ loves the church. In Mark chapter 12:33 He says, *"Love your neighbor the way you love yourself."* A marriage is a union between two people creating a bond in which their souls are knitted together. Then how can he or why would he ever want to get away from her? We must control our competitive edge or it will drive a wedge between us. Even though this is a marriage, ladies we are individual people and sometimes our self-satisfaction raises its ugly head. The word "away" may seem to be a negative title for this chapter, but if we look for a positive context we can bring a different outlook. Without a positive context, negative phrases may take hold of us and lead women to an unprofitable relationship.

I may speak and refer to this principle looking from the outside into my own relationship. For a relationship to remain viable, vital, and productive we must not walk in the ways of the wicked. Women by nature are more vocal than men. It is not my speech that turns him away from me. It is the way I administer it to him. More specifically, this topic brings to mind Proverbs 21:9. It refers to a man who retreats to a corner in the house rather than contend with a contentious woman. This is a negative version of getting away from your wife. This literally means that a man removed himself from the presence of his wife due to the way she is behaving. We can't allow this fear to dictate how we interact with one another.

To get a positive result we must always look for a spiritual application from our Maker. The word "way" is used to describe a manner of life or the direction to a purpose. In the book of John chapter 14:6 Jesus says, *"I am the way, the truth, and the life, no man cometh to the father, but by me."* In Proverbs 21:2, the Bible also says that every way of a man is right in his own eyes. The "way" is usually wrapped up in our soul's personality. My way is my living example on how I perform that which I believe in. We are to deny the way we feel and approach God through His way. We must be truthful with one another even if it sometimes hurts. My husband and I made our covenant of purpose with this theme in mind and refuse to debate that which is good for us.

There has to be a change in direction and personality when a couple seeks their purpose in serving the Lord. They both must agree and request a-way of perfection from each other. For example; when a man and woman gets married they vow their ways of service to each other, in sickness and in health, for richer or poorer, and until death do ye part. You will find that God unveils attributes of those who He is well-pleased with so that we will become favorable examples to follow. When the Lord puts favor in your life a blessing beyond comprehension shall follow. To prosper, the husband must get a-way from his wife. This may require change and sacrifice on both parts, mainly the woman because she exhibits the most influential spirit in the home.

My husband needed to get a-way from me. It may require me to be brutally honest, and sometimes a meek and quiet spirit is needed. In 1 Peter chapter 3, the Bible encourages women to present a winning way to lead her husband to the Lord. Many times our ways speak louder than our words. Women often use the phrase "I am a strong woman" but the strongest women in the world are the meekest women, because they are able to control the strength and power she has within her soul. I needed to exhibit a-way that we both can cleave to.

When my way is pleasing to God, my companion becomes the beneficiary of my blessings and I'm the recipient of his blessings. When I examine things that came to pass, I found that as we grew, our challenges changed and my ways matured in wisdom. When we are older our ways should become a pattern and a gift for others to follow giving God the glory. He comes to get a-way from me and I set my "way" before the presence of the Lord. I have an equal share in the responsibility and the blessing of the home. Getting a-way from me helps us both to fill whatever is lacking in our purpose together. My ways have a profound effect on my family. God reminds us in the first chapter of the book of Haggai to examine ourselves to see if we are abiding in the faith. He tells me to, *"Consider my ways"*. When things are not going the way I think they should, I must examine whether or not God is withholding my blessings because of my ways.

I have a plate full of needs and God wants to supply them all, but He may have one thing against me. God gives me all things pertaining to life and godliness according to the perfect law of liberty. I can't blame God if my way and receipt for life doesn't work. For example, my mother can cook cabbage that will melt in your mouth and my husband loves it. I wanted to please my husband so I asked her to teach me the way she prepares it. After she gave me the recipe and showed me how to make it, I began to prepare it. However, if it doesn't turn out right, I need to consider where I went wrong. Every action that we have has a process to it. In the Bible, Abraham and Sarah both had roles to play in the plan of God. God later praises her for the way she reverenced Abraham in I Peter chapter 3.

The way we communicate to our spouse should be far better than our beginning. The roles are different but we are strategically placed in a position to best serve each other. Service is something that we often fail to do and when it goes undone we pay the ultimate price. There are disappointing times with Sarah and Abraham, because providing a-way for each other's purpose may not have immediate results. We may retreat and rely on our own physical talent. Sarah was a beautiful woman. How would I know that? Because when God saves a space in His word to describe how a king set his eyes on her beauty, you better believe she is beyond a diva.

In today's lifestyle someone with her show stopping beauty could easily fall into the hype and think she could walk on water. Sarah could have easily been in a king's concubine and lavishly taken care of. Sarah knew her purpose and gave Abraham her way of reverence for all to see from the very beginning. She was aware that Abraham's children would be numbered as the stars in heaven and she would be the benchmark in that process. Our purpose together should develop one mind in executing God's plan. The way we care for each other is not only meant for us, but for the world to see also.

Marriage should be like a city on top of a hill for all to see as they pass by. Our example should inspire people to say 'show me the way' to having a great relationship. Unfortunately today many observers are wagging their heads as they pass by saying in their hearts *I can do bad all by myself.* Marriage is a beautiful thing, but sometimes it's made up of people with mismatch ways. You can't hitch a mule and a bull to the same plow wagon because they will always be at odds with one another. Don't allow others to label you as the new odd couple. Two people cannot travel this life together unless they agree on each other's destination. There must be a covenant made concerning the way you treat each other. The way he should love you, and the way you should respect each other. Those are the two attributes of the Spirit, which are our code of ethics, and provides a recipe for a great marriage.

The Bible says, "See that I reverence my husband," meaning make every effort to establish it as a true saying in the home. The way we interact in the home is dependent on our obedience in our roles. When he loves me he demonstrates it by putting my well-being before his. I provide a way for him to love me and he provides a way for me to love him. A woman's righteous ways are better than gold and the beauty of her reverence is worthy of praise.

Let's Talk: Woman to Woman

There is only one of you and no one has your way of doing things. You are superior in the field of your man. Your way never goes unnoticed by God. To be honest, there was a time when I said "there is no way a man would ever rule my house", but God made a way out of my no way.

How many ways have you improved your relationships? Explain

_____
_____
_____
_____
_____
_____
_____

Which of your ways needs consideration?

_____
_____
_____
_____
_____
_____
_____

What Truth has this stone given you? Explain:

_____
_____
_____
_____
_____
_____
_____

Am I like a woman known as Moses' wife Ziporah?

What is marriage? It is a love between a man and wife. What happens in between is really the issue. Ziporah, like any woman, vows to love Moses for better or for worse, in sickness, in health, and for richer or poorer. The vow of the husband's wife should also include "in their purpose" because it is the man's role to help his wife in her purpose also.

Following the purpose of another may cause serious alterations in your life. It seemed that Moses and Ziporah do not share the same religious belief. Oftentimes the man of God receives instruction from the Lord and his wife has to trust and follow. Secondhand faith may require a stronger commitment by the woman. She must also put her trust in the person delivering the message. In this case the wife can be a help or a hindrance to her husband. When Ziporah realized that Moses was going to Egypt and his sons had to be circumcised by the order of God she lashed out at him calling him a bloody man. Before we do anything for God we must present our bodies a living sacrifice holy and acceptable before we begin our reasonable service to him. She didn't understand that Moses was only fulfilling one of the most historic events in the history of mankind, which involved leading the children of Israel out of Egypt. We find out later that Moses had to send his wife Ziporah back to her father's house because she could not see beyond the discomfort of her children.

It is difficult for a man to fulfill what God has called him to do if his wife refuses to be a stimulus that helps him succeed in his purpose. This requires her to be actively involved with his ministry. There is not much written about Ziporah, but there is much to learn.

During the 40 years in the wilderness you hear little or nothing about Ziporah, only that the people were upset that Moses married an Ethiopian woman. It is difficult to walk with your husband outside your comfort zone. A wife's duty is not merely to be a spouse, but to stand with him through his victories as well as his defeats. When you read of Moses remember his wife is present when they murmured against him. She probably had to endure the hatred from the Hebrew people. When God calls married men to his purpose, the wife becomes part of the deal. It is no guarantee that she will cooperate or finish the course with him. There will come a period when it looks like he doesn't have a clue in what he is doing and you are fed up. This is a stressor in your purpose that can pull you apart. Before you know it one is giving up and the other is taken down.

There is a growing temptation for women to take the kids and run. Even though there is limited information about Ziporah she is no different than women today. She is following Moses on a wing and a prayer. Can you imagine the conversations they had each night when Moses returns to the tent to sleep? Instead of a three-day journey to the Promise Land, she has to spend 40 years in the wilderness due to the disobedience of others. Traveling through unknown territory filled with scorpions, hostile enemies, lack of water, lack of food, and no GPS signal. Like other husbands, Moses could only say each night, "Baby we're almost there."

Let's Talk: Woman to Woman

The man is the stronger vessel, but there is weakness inside. The woman is the weaker vessel, but she has the strength inside to endure the weights put on the family. Behind every great man who fights for his purpose there is a woman taking his punches also.

How can a behavior like Delilah hinder your purpose?

_____
_____
_____
_____
_____
_____
_____
_____

What truth did you learn from this stone?

_____
_____
_____
_____
_____
_____
_____
_____

The Headless Woman

There have been many recessions throughout the history of our society. We very seldom relate a recession to moral behavior. Godly values and virtuous behavior is dramatically diminishing in this progressive culture. Before we hit the wall let's sit down and have a chat, woman to woman. This may be a touchy subject for women who have been abandoned by their fathers or their husbands. We all have experienced some type of male rejection. So permit me to use my personal trial and testimony.

In the quest to advance my life and career, I had to ask myself did I leave anything behind. I know the majority of us grow up and we leave home and move about to our own place, our own rules, build our own family, etc. But upon leaving did I forget to pack my head? I know many of us consider ourselves to be "independent" (including myself at one time), but does this behavior seem to be more of a revolution today than that of a positive behavior? The word "independent" refers to one who is not subject to the control of others. She is not subordinate to the will of another. Is it unpopular to be a woman who follows or honors God's initial plan?

Women may feel more comfortable in the protective class that America has constitutionally formed. By no means am I condemning single parent homes. I was deeply rooted in the single parenting process with 2 beautiful daughters, because like some of you, I was left to do what men should have done. Single parenting is a 24 hours, 7 days a week occupation with no days off. The only problem I created in showcasing this lifestyle is that I began to give myself the credit for my success. It doesn't matter if I leave my father's house or separate from the house of my former husband, the Lord continues to be on top as the head of where I live. I am to never go headless through this life. I know it looks glamorous to be on your own, but the woman who loves the Lord never wants to be without Him. The impact of this type of recession is uncertain, but for sure it does not concur with God's model. Unfortunately, this model for many is hard to accept because it seems like a set back into the dark ages.

We remember that through history women have been raped, domestically abused, socially and economically rejected with no civil recourse. Their afflictions were mostly administered by the hands of men. For this cause, American women, have a growing disdain for the position and the legal legislative authority of the man. There is a vanishing confidence in men that has left many women to live in this headless rebellion that seems to be born out of a social dysfunction. There is a growing number of women who opted out and choose to exist under their own rule. I know these stones may be slippery and hard to cross over, but without the headship of the Father your challenges will only become greater.

The Bible tells us in the book of Psalms chapter 127, *"Except the Lord build the house, they labour in vain that build it; except the Lord keep the city, the watchman waketh but in vain."* You are so right ladies' men have failed in their roles, but not all. The statistics of failures are staggering and getting worse with each generation. Do I run wild and unruly because others have failed? We may not say it but many believe God's methods are outdated. The more Satan uses us to promote ourselves as self- made, the less we believe. Heading a house as a single parent is usually never the intention of woman, but through cause and effect it's the hand that she's dealt. When you put your money on the man who is not ready you get the responsibility of the house.

In each biblical dispensation the woman's headship of authority was never uncovered. Really no one's head is uncovered. In the book of I Corinthians 11, scripture says that the head of Christ is God, the head of man is Christ, and the head of a woman is man and the head of children is parents. This does not mean she is second class in God's eyesight, for we abide in our head and our head in us. She is a companion of man. She came out of him and he comes out of her. Ladies you need a head to judge a head. Even though I had a house and lived on my own I took my man before my respected head. My father was deceased, but my oldest brother who I respected was still living. He would inspect, observe and give me the honest report on things I cannot see in a man. I am not exempt, my husband did the same. If a man resists inspection he may have work about him that is unfinished which he refuses to reveal to you. Don't apologize for this, do it on purpose, inspect him. I can't tell you how many times I've heard women including myself say "I wish I knew then what I know now. Be careful ladies without God's chain of command a headless woman is just spinning her wheels.

Let's Talk: Woman to Woman

I, like you, was doing just fine. I was a product of America's success story. Had my own house, two children, a great job, educated, physically in my prime, and business motivated. "What do I need a man for," I thought. All these things are not mine but the Lord. We must learn to put all things under His feet and make Him the Head of your house as a woman, a wife, or a widow.

Do you live your life without a head?

_____
_____
_____
_____
_____

Are you under a headship or are you headless?

What truth has this stone given me? Explain:

Am I like a woman known as Jezebel?

I have met a countless number of women in my lifetime. I have been to women retreats, conventions, and sporting events all over this nation. I can't recall running into anyone who's name was Jezebel. No mother wanted to name her child after this notorious woman. Maybe it's because that name comes with a negative reputation or it may cause others to believe you are able to live up to it. People would often say that names can't hurt you. This saying may be true but a name can most definitely mark you.

There are only two women named Jezebel mentioned in the Bible. One woman is found in the book of revelation and is guilty of seducing the servants in the church at Thyatira to commit fornication, and to eat things sacrificed unto idols. Her name is most commonly used to describe a woman with an unruly sexual behavior. She poses as a prophetess and is publicly allowed to have sex with the brethren of the assembly. Jesus praised the church for their work, but ridiculed them for their weakness and tolerance of her wickedness. Since no one was bold enough to stand against her God pronounces his own sentencing against her and all who committed adultery with her.

In recent years our behaviors have become more transparent. We have boldness where our sexuality is exploited without shame. This story isn't unique or an isolated event in biblical history. The name Jezebel today is usually associated with someone who is viewed as a home wrecker. The church is filled with ordinary people and has its share of seductresses. It is a sad thing to live a life where no one wants to be called by your name. The other woman named Jezebel is found in the book I Kings chapter 21. She is the wife of Ahab, the King of Judah and a queen who didn't know her place in the kingdom. She was conniving with a dangerous temper, and had a reputation that caused men to run with fear. She abused the power of her husband and used it for her own wicked purpose. She had no respect for the king, the leadership, or any prophet of the Almighty God. Jezebel had Naboth the Jezreelite killed, stole his vineyard, and threaten to kill Elijah the prophet also.

Jezebel is a woman who lives by her own rules and breaks commandments without care. She is a woman who does not take no for an answer. To reject her request would often mean a plot against you or immediate death. Once God cursed her, she was dead while she lived. She was separated from the Spirit of God and her soul had been required. In the book of II Kings 9:36 God said that the dogs shall eat Jezebel by the wall of Jezreel God himself pronounced a sentence of death upon Jezebel and did not allow her carcass to be recognized after she fell. The problem with Jezebel is that she encouraged King Ahab (her husband) to do wickedness in the sight of the Lord. She was the hen who pecks her husband's every move.

A woman should never disrespect the manner of God's ordained leadership. We can definitely see that God was upset with the way both women slice and diced the men in their lives. I believe she may have been spoiled or use to getting her way. If Jezebel lived today which word would we use to describe her as a person? To sum it up we would probably say she's crazy because she is unstable and very uncomfortable to be around. Being referred to by any name defining a negative characteristic is not good because it can take a lifetime to live it down.

You and I may not be named Jezebel, but what do people call us to describe our identity to others? I have met many people called by the oddest names, some to compliment and some to discredit. I knew a young woman who people use to call 'Alley Cat'. This was not her birth name. She was given this name because of the location she was found having sex with men. When she was older she rejected this name, but continually ran into people who referred to her by the name "Alley Cat". I could see the remorse and the shame in her eyes especially when she ran into those men. I pray that we never let people chain us to our past. The Lord can make you a new creature in Christ Jesus and old things will pass away and all things will become new. To develop a new name may require you to seek new relationships.

Let's Talk: Woman to Woman

Jezebel refused to reign as a queen under the leadership of the king. She also had a blatant disregard for the prophets who spoke the word of God. Her wicked imagination was set on destroying any man who defied her request for anything. She possesses a Dr. Jekyll and Mr. Hyde personality that flips at a switch. When you think about it, a lot of women today should have been named Jezebel.

Can acting like Jezebel hinder your purpose? How?

_____
_____
_____
_____
_____
_____
_____
_____
_____

Do you have behaviors like Jezebel that follows you?

_____
_____
_____

Safe Deposit Box

The sweetest part in the life of a woman is her place of deposit. She is a fertile ground which breeds an intimate commitment from the man. God uses the word trust as a transferable enchantment that is put in a place only He can reach. The book of Proverbs describes a woman who defines the word virtue in several categories. One specific attribute is trust. It is a quality that everyone possesses and will eventually share with another person for safe keeping.

In today's society it is evident that the covenant of trust is shattered more than any other part of a man's spirit. That's right my sister, it is a spiritual thing. Even when the relationship between a man and a woman dissolves, the root of the problem is the violation of trust. Although the relationship is salvaged the hardest thing to restore is the other person's mistrust. The book of Psalms has 50 scriptures spoken by David that mentions the value of his trust and where it should lie. In God is where he puts his trust, but what about us? We have to deal with trust on a daily basis. We trust that we are getting paid on Friday, we trust that the food we paid for was properly prepared, we trust that our children are safe where we left them, and we trust that our houses are still standing when we return home.

What is it about this woman in Proverbs 31, and what can I learn from her? The first thing that I learned from her is that I must have myself together. My life must be as stable as Fort Knox. Why would I put my money in the bank? First, I must have a level of faith that the institution is capable of keeping that which is valuable to me. Secondly, the bank's reputation is at risk if they lose or mishandle my money. Finally, I must have a record of receipt that verifies my daily or weekly deposits with protection and recompense for any theft. So I can't lose.

In Proverbs Chapter 31:11 the scriptures say that her husband doth "safely" trust in her. She keeps an account of his deposit and, the husband has a complete confidence in her virtue to hold his investments. I know we have been programmed to say we can't trust a man, because many of us have been robbed of our emotional tithes that we put into unguarded relationships. When you work to build your trust where will you store it, under your mattress? There is no interest under a mattress. Your interest is always in another person. In the book of John chapter 13:34-35, Jesus tells his disciples to love one another as I have loved you. If they keep this love then all men will know that they are disciples of Jesus. There is no better interest than that.

Our society parades mistrust against these principles through media, movies, and even marriage. I know it is better to give than to receive but is it better to trust or be trusted? I not only want to be trusted, but have a trust that is safe. Can he deposit his fears, dreams, his well-being, faults and his love in me? I first have to ask my God for wisdom and His protection around my safe deposit box. His valuables are entrusted in me for safe keeping. A breach in martial confidentiality may be the very reason there is little trust and little wealth in many marriages. When your spouse deposits his spiritual wealth in your spirit you magnify your relationship with God to others.

Another verse, Proverbs 31:12, *"She will do him good and not evil."* Can a good woman do evil? Can an evil woman do good? Which one does a man want? To tell the truth, both sound unstable. In the relationship the man provides the ship, you are the anchor of that ship. Your confidence in each other is groomed over a period of time, through trials and testing. I wish I could tell you that trust comes easy, but it doesn't. Many have laid a portion of their trust at the wrong doorstep while others became bankrupt and couldn't put their trust in anyone else. Trust is not to be squandered nor spent unwisely. My safety box is my vault and I hold the key to all that he gives me.

Let's Talk: Woman to Woman

A covenant between me and thee is not to be taken lightly. No one will give me their goods if the deposit box is unsecured. I cannot serve if I can't be trusted. For, if we guard the trust given to us we will receive a blessing far above more than we can ask for.

Is the trust of others safe with you? Explain:

_____
_____
_____
_____
_____

Has mistrust altered your purpose?

_____
_____
_____
_____
_____

What truth has this stone given you?

_____
_____

_____
_____
_____
_____

Am I like a woman known as Rahab?

God has charged his women to be the keeper in her house. In the book of Joshua, Chapter 2, Rahab's house is transformed from a place of sexual immorality to a place of safety, and a safe house, for God's agents. The victory of the Lord will often come through the covenant we establish in our house. We would have never chosen Rahab's house as a house of safety, because it represents a public penthouse. Men, at one time, were looked upon as tools for her profit. Joshua sent men to spy on the land before the Israelites army would come to overthrow the city of Jericho. The men came by night and entered the house of the harlot named Rahab. She hid them on the top of the roof of the house. Word got out that there were spies within the walls and the authorities were notified to search the city. When Rahab's house was searched, the king sent an order to Rahab that she should turn over the spies in her house but Rahab kept her word even if it meant she would suffer.

Rahab knew that they were men of God and not the kind of men that frequent her house in the past. These men were vital to the existence of her and her household. Her house became a safety box and security exchange covenant between her and those that dwelled with her. Rahab assured the men that she would keep the covenant they established. She could have easily been rewarded for turning them in at the king's request. Rahab understood that no amount of money would save her from the destruction to come. Her conviction rested on three things.

She first exhibited a promise and a trust that no matter what I will keep thee. She hides them in the most secure or secret place in her house, and redirects any danger that threatens their lives. Secondly, she is encouraged by what she has heard of them. A man's reputation plays a vital role in developing a personal relationship with a woman. Rahab knows their promise, their victories and their faith in God. Thirdly, she must know who his God is. A woman should always beware of the god the man brings into the house. Whatever he falls down to worship must be able to divinely lift him up but only the Lord is able to do this.

Rahab's house sat on top of the wall that surrounded the city of Jericho. But the Lord tells Joshua to march around the city one time each day for six days and seven times on the seventh day. God tells the priest to blow their trumpets, the people to shout, and the wall will fall flat down. If the wall falls shouldn't Rahab's house fall also? How can God keep His promise when everything is going to fall apart in a few days? Rahab not only has concern for herself, but her family which is in her house under a command not to leave. The wall of Jericho fell flat but Rahab's house stood firm and all who took shelter inside were safe. The Lord has promised to bless us richly if we hold fast to our purpose in Him. The Lord knows how to sanctify your house and set us apart from all that surrounds us. Whose promise is your house standing on?

The book of Joshua chapter 2:12 teaches us that there is a security exchange. She says, *"Swear unto me by the Lord; since I have showed you kindness show me also kindness."* It also teaches us that there should be a true token of my promise to you. Rahab had an opportunity to advance her career by betraying her commitment to the two men, but instead she hung a scarlet thread out her window as a symbol which binds her oath with the man who returned to her house.

Let's Talk: Woman to Woman

Like Rahab, my scarlet thread erases what my house use to be. "It now stands on a covenant between me and thee"

What promise is your house standing on?

_____
_____
_____
_____
_____
_____
_____
_____

How can the covenant like Rahab help you to fulfill your purpose?

_____
_____
_____
_____
_____
_____
_____
_____

Five Phases of
A Woman

The ideal description of Proverbs' anonymous lady is something women have been trying to achieve since the beginning of time. It takes courage to be a woman who can live with the core values mentioned in Proverbs 31. Life is hard enough, but without God it's a road that has no light at the end of the tunnel. The fad today is not to be virtuous, but to be contentious. That is a woman waiting to display outburst to prove she is something or someone to be reckoned with. We can find her on every block, radio, television show, club, and even church. Try to find a virtuous woman; she is not in your common place, and by the way, you don't want to be a person that anybody can find. Only a special man searches for a woman with virtue. He knows God has anointed her and the gift that she possesses cannot be denied.

In the past, discount stores would be overstocked with unsellable items that needed to be pulled from the shelf. These products would eventually be advertised in a scrap bin with a posted sign that says a dime for a dozen. We are a peculiar people and without a heavenly sign we become like everybody else. I don't have anything against Facebook or Instagram, but please don't advertise yourself in the "everything must go" sales page. This is where we find who we are not looking for. The most valuable things on earth are things which are not found in common places. I don't believe I have ever seen a ruby because this is a precious and rare jewel which is kept under a guard.

A good (godly) man looks for a woman with a virtuous quality, because Proverbs12:4 says, *she is a crown to her husband.* Rubies are pennies compared to the crown that she bestows on him. She represents his royalty and dignity, but a shameless woman is a cancer to the man she is with. Secondly, can she be trusted with the purpose God has given him? Does she reassure her husband each day that she has his back and will support him in times of trouble. Her wisdom erases the fear of any social or financial loss that could threaten their relationship. Proverbs chapter 8 says" *that knowledge is more precious than gold and wisdom is better than rubies"*. A woman's wisdom is a priceless ornament which comes straight out of heaven. God did not make us with cheap material that depreciates or goes out of style. Her physical age may bring blemishes, but when her spiritual nature matures it is cleansed of any spots or wrinkles. She should never spend the substance of her youth in riotous living. Remember don't burn all your fire for the devil and blow smoke in God's face. She should always avoid places where women are viewed as cheap.

Thirdly, my house is my sanctuary. It is a dwelling that is departmentalized for the physical and spiritual growth of his purpose. The woman is the keeper of the house and the man ruleth it with all gravity. When I choose my house I examine each department. Though it is a physical dwelling it plays an important role in the security of the household and marriage. We first make sure that the foundation which it stands on is secure. The kitchen is the place where she gives meat to her household. Her restroom is a place of solitude and hygiene preparation for her personal appearance. Her living room is used for the hospitality of friends, especially those in the household of the Lord. Her bedroom is her sanctuary where she and her mate have intimate adoration. She is entrusted with the resources of the home. Her husband is her first, her family next, and then cometh her business and her God is above all, through all and in all that she has.

In many homes if this is not the priority list it will cause a confusion that God cannot bless. She manages her inventory and is known among the merchants in her area. She is not a busy body but about her business. She is rich in faith and takes pride in building her reputation before her children and society. She will be like a tree planted by the rivers of water and God will bless her with the fruit of His Spirit in due season. Her leaf also shall not wither and whatsoever she doeth shall prosper.

Let's Talk: Woman to Woman

God has set a bar for you. It doesn't mean you will live a perfect life; no one does. Strength (virtue) and honor is the garment that she wears daily. Her children will rise up and not chastise her, but they will bless her in the days to come. You must excel the status quo. The bar is too low and the penalty for a perverse woman is too high.

Do you discount your values to fit into society?

_____
_____
_____
_____
_____
_____
_____

Does your phase make your house a home?

_____
_____
_____
_____

What truth has this stone given you? Explain:

Am I like a woman known as a strange woman?

We have been blessed to learn vital lessons in life that we can pass on to our sons and daughters (sons in particular). We know because the road that they are on we probably traveled it several times. We often remind them when they are traveling their road to never pick up hitch hikers. We tell them this in hopes of avoiding or solving the problems that will surely come one day in their life. But this advice most likely creates another problem that every child faces and that is curiosity. I felt it necessary to speak with my sisters who have sons. It may seem that I'm talking to a son, but I am talking through the eyes of every mother that has a son. God has always warned his sons not to marry the daughter of men, because they will turn your heart away from the Lord. As a mother of a young man you may spend your time monitoring a suitable match for him, but one day it happens he walks in with a hitch hiker. A hitch hiker is a stranger who wants to ride along with you. The stranger is only half packed, but says they are going the same way you're going. The stranger will ride for a moment but won't go the distance with you. I write this for all mothers who know the motive of the strange woman and want the best for her son.

In the book of Genesis chapter 26, 27, Rebekah, the wife of Isaac, pleaded with her sons that they take not a wife of the Canaanites. Her son Esau disobeyed her request and took unto him two wives of the Hittites and two wives of the Canaanites. His wives and their gods became a grievous burden to Isaac and Rebekah. The home became more disjointed because Esau chose to be defiant and married women who walked not with the Lord. An in-law can make a once livable home into a strange and lowly place.

In the book of Proverbs chapter 5, there is a woman without a name. Her description overshadows her family name and she is only referred to as a "strange woman." The word strange doesn't mean she possess a physical defect. Often times her beauty is so compelling it blinds the man and doesn't allow him to see his fall from grace.

Proverbs says her words are sensual and arouses the prey she is after. What started out as passionate intimacy in the beginning becomes bitter as worms. Her ways are un-stable, her intent is without remorse, her price is too much and she will deliver you to Satan's front door when she is finished. You will enjoy her for only a short while. God created this woman and her beauty but he tells you not to look upon, touch, nor handle her. Like the tree in the garden, once you eat of it you shall surely die.

We all know a strange woman or have once been on the border line flirting with this type of deception. Be thou an example to thy son and give instruction that teaches him to avoid the imperfect match especially with the woman who will not change her ways, but rather boast of her dishonesty. Just as light and darkness cannot exist together in the same room a son of God and a strange woman have no fellowship together. They are set against each other. Hear me now my son you cannot win. You may attempt to change her foolish ways, but she will rape your mind and leave it void of understanding. There will be no blessing to the family; she is not an in-law, she is Satan's outlaw. Deliver yourself from the snares of her words, and lust not after her beauty.

Let's Talk: Woman to Woman

Show your sons all the strong men who were made simple and brought down to a piece of bread.

Have past relationships caused you to develop strange ways?

How can a strange woman behavior hinder your purpose?

All the Single Ladies

It's a known fact that for years, women have always played by the rules and didn't complain so tell me **why are there so many single women today**? Society and the media try to put the blame all on us, but I beg to disagree. Our desire for marriage is generally persuaded by the first married couple we see. This is usually our mom and dad. The home was created to be the training camp to instruct children how to leave father and mother and cleave to our own mate. God's spiritual order still encourages women to marry, bear children, and be a keeper at home in that order. What happened to that order? In today's culture, those days have passed and what remains is an order of multiple choices. The dysfunctions of men today have also played a role in that demise.

The book of Ephesians chapter 5 speaks of the man as the head of the wife and that he gives himself for her. In our world today "who's giving" and "who's giving up"? Some women may not be ready for this type of relationship. Some may be scorned never to do it again. You may be down for the count but don't throw in the towel. Choosing a man is like a box of chocolates. Some are smooth and creamy and some are assorted nuts. It's a woman desire to find a good man, raise great kids, and have a respectful home. Remember, a good man's footsteps are ordered by God. It seems there has been a serious breakdown in the quality of available men. The pool is dwindling and men have become so socially scattered that you never know who you are getting,

I once asked a man would he marry a woman who had been incarcerated, on drugs, an alcoholic, children fathered by four different men, domestically violent, uneducated, disrespectful, broke, mix sexual identity, doesn't take care of her children or home, won't go to work/or has an extended adolescence behavior. He quickly stated "not a chance". So why would we as women marry a man with those same issues? I rest my case. Please don't misunderstand me because there are good and God fearing men out there who are not in Satan's snares.

Here are a few tips for the honest and weary seekers who want a spiritual mate. Those who are merely looking for a warm body to lie beside need not apply. Ask the Lord to prepare you as a woman for younger ladies to imitate. You won't have to find a man, he will find you; but you must try his spirit, not his shell (body) or resources (money), because neither can bring you happiness.

The Bible, in I John chapter 4:1 says, *"Try the spirit to see whether it is sent of God."* What's the test? First, if you have to entice him to go to church keep looking. God won't send you someone He has not prepared. Adam was already prepared when God brought Eve to him. He knew the word of God, had a place of employment and a residence. Many women say you don't have to marry a man of God to have a good marriage. You are right, if this world is your only destination.

Secondly, I have encountered many women who rolled the dice and took a chance with an unstable mate. They became imprison in the battle of his demonic behavior. It is our responsibility to pierce through false fables that target young people. Listen close, Jesus said if you love me keep my commandments. These three words *I love you* have been spoken more than any other words in history. When a man tells you this what do you say? Don't melt make him explain.

It's very important to watch for signs. Does he only act like a man when it's convenient? Does he only use these false morals to attract me and capture my heart? However, when the play is over, the scene is cut, and the real person emerges, I realize I have entangled my soul with a hypocrite. My son had a classmate (a young lady) who dated a young man when she was in high school and he became psychotically infatuated with her. She tried to break it off but it only made him furious and he restrained her in his house. He became so enraged that he began to cut her into pieces and all the while crying, "I loved you". Be careful about men who say they are crazy in love with you. Notice the first word, "CRAZY", it may mean don't ever try to leave me.

To find a man doesn't mean to stumble upon him or to seek him at night. Choosing the right man should never be by accident. He should be always ready to prove himself. Is he adding temperance to control his actions? Is he adding godliness to know that he is under the authority of God and not himself? Is he adding love so that he will love me as Christ loved the Church? You won't find a saint, but you must find one who is making these investments to transform his old self. The word find is also a word used after a judge makes a ruling after seeking the truth concerning an individual. The book of Proverbs chapter 18:22 states that whosoever finds a wife finds a good thing. The word wife is a noun and a verb at the same time. She holds the title of wife and her actions proves it beyond doubt. Single ladies, it is who you are and what you do that makes you a good thing.

Some of you may have the gift and have a comfort within yourself to live alone. Sometimes we think that single women are only women who have never been married, but there are single women who are divorced, and widowed. Some are looking to marry again and some say once is enough for them. Whatever state you're in remember to go forward. Patiently wait on the Lord and he will renew your strength. Oftentimes the best part and most productive part of your life happen when you are alone. You are able to prepare and heal yourself for the next phase without interruption. Do not waste your time in your single life. When you are single you possess a better confidence, because there is no male safety net only you and the Lord. Explore your innovative spirit and get closer to the Lord and He will direct your footsteps. Take time to restore your virtue and be ready for the day that God shows himself strong in your life, and you'll see that he saved the best for last.

Let's Talk: Woman to Woman

Be careful not to change the course of your life by choosing someone going another direction with a sign that says, ***"Follow me"***.

What type of man are you waiting on?

_____
_____
_____
_____
_____
_____

What preparations are you making while you wait?

_____
_____
_____
_____
_____
_____

What truth has this stone given you?

_____
_____
_____
_____
_____
_____

Am I like the woman caught in adultery?

One Sunday morning during the close of worship, the preacher extended the invitation and a young lady walked forward. She was moved by the sermon and came down front with tears on her face. I believe she was carrying a load too heavy for her to bear and needed the prayers of the righteous. During her statement she repented and stated that she had committed fornication. There was a gasp in the auditorium. Why? I'm pretty sure, and almost positive, that she wasn't the only one in that assembly who had committed fornication. This may be the reason many young women are carrying around burdens, because they cannot find the merciful to obtain mercy.

In the book of John chapter 8, a crowd of people caught a woman in the very act of adultery and led her to Jesus. It is believed that these witnesses had evil intentions from the very start. She was arrested by this mob and may have even been taken without being allowed to get dressed. We sometimes over react with insensitivity and add shame on top of shame. Remember when a sister is overtaken in a fault, those who are spiritual should restore such a one in the spirit of meekness. Most of all, remember to consider your ways and don't be a fornicator condemning a fornicator. This is social media before its time.

Obviously the accusers made the event public and a crowd of bystanders quickly grew. They put her before Jesus to have His take on it. Whenever our minds are set on catching something or someone we lay a snare to trap them. We know the whereabouts and the location of the prey. Jesus does not have private detectives employed to catch sinners and bring them to Him. Our Lord has given some to be apostles, some prophets, some evangelist, some pastors, and some teachers, but I never read of some catchers as a work in the ministry. If that's your ministry stop it. There is nothing spiritual about it.

In the book of John chapter 8, it speaks of a crowd of people witnessing the sin of adultery. Was it their duty to make it public or to handle it privately? To help one another as sisters we must remember that all have sinned but all saints haven't been caught by the crowd. Many people are incarcerated, but there are more criminals at large, than there are behind bars. The beautiful thing about this tragedy is that my forgiveness is not in the hands of the crowd, but the hands of the Lord. The woman is oftentimes the one who bears the proof of this act, especially if she becomes pregnant. All eyes are on her and she shares an unequal penalty in this fault. People who accuse and judge you will only bring their sins to light. My sisters go and sin no more because we all have been there.

Let's Talk: Woman to Woman

We don't condone it, but you are not the only one wrong. It takes two to tangle so there is a partner who escaped with the record of our very act.

How can you rebound from adultery?

_____
_____
_____
_____
_____
_____

Have you ever been publicly humiliated? If so explain why:

_____
_____

_____
_____
_____
_____

The Hamburger Helper

When you rise in the morning and look in the mirror what do you see? Will you see God's most beautiful creation in human life or the creation of a life that was once beautiful? Your mirror will show you that our days are short. What do we have to show for it? Have I been about my Father's business? For this cause I am re-examining what I do and whether it is profitable for me or costing days of my life with no compensation. Many will testify in fear that we pay the price for procrastination and there is no refund. Satan has convinced many women that the one who we are made from is our enemy. This is not true. God has put enmity between the woman and the serpent, not the man. Satan has put himself in the man whom I am purposed to help. It makes it easy for me to reject him. But it is God's word that gives me comfort and understanding. I find myself in private prayer asking God for better understanding of difficult points of purpose.

I have heard many sermons but there are two in particular that I recall hearing the most, and that is Psalms 23 and Ephesians 5:23. Ephesians 5:23 is the one that caused me to grit my teeth at one time because; I thought it meant I had to relinquish control of my life to someone else. I believe some women may have remained single because they misunderstood this passage. If you are not seeking God's purpose it may seem like it is attempting to put us back under the old law. It is often facilitated by a man and rolled into a 30-minute sermon. Afterwards we become entangled in a war with our spirit to submit to the dominance of this passage.

I will tell you, truthfully, it was hard sometimes because this scripture in the hands of the wrong man is not a good thing. We need God to intervene and set this crooked road straight that has redirected many unsuspecting women. If I believe there is a God I have to believe all things are true especially my purpose that breaths in Him. Everything that God made has a helper. Every beast has a helper to reproduce, just like the flowers need rain, and the earth needs the sun, so why would I think my man would not need a helper?

Do you remember the commercial introducing the product Hamburger Helper? The products and spices which are added to it help it become more than just a bowl of meat. The spices helped give it a better taste, aroma, and sustaining power to have leftovers for another day. God has made the woman with a spice and flavor fit for a man. When God sprinkles me on him, his taste buds water, his stomach growls, and he praise me with favor. Go through any fast food drive thru and ask for a plain hamburger and I promise you the attendant will respond "with nothing on it?" When you get to the window you will only receive two slices of bread and a piece of meat. God saw man like that plain hamburger with nothing on it. It wasn't good served alone. My mission is to spice up the purpose that we share together. God doesn't want man to be plain, medium, or rare; He wants him "well done".

I learned to love my purpose because God's love is in it. My husband won't be my husband forever because there is no marriage in heaven, but while he is mine, it is my purpose to add my ingredients to this lonely burger. He will present himself to God on our behalf like a whopper fully loaded with extra cheese. It doesn't matter how well you are doing; the truth is everyone needs a helper. Like the hamburger helper, he is made for serving so that others can taste of what the Lord has made. He is an offering to God's purpose and how I respond to him has a lasting aroma in our covenant. In the book of Job chapters 1, and 2, the Bible says that the Lord puts his servant into the hand of Satan for testing.

The devil was allowed to strip Job of the things that seasoned his life. He finally reduced Job to a sore infested shell of a man. Satan promised to turn Job's heart from God and make him curse Him to his face. It seemed that through his sorrow and sufferings Satan had his bull's eye on his man, but Job wasn't the real target.

His wife attempts to season him with a vile flavor to curse God to His face and die. She wanted to tempt Job to say something that she really wants to say herself. Is she a helper or a thorn in his flesh trying to separate him from God? A wife must face the fact that she is a part of the husband's trials whether she likes it or not. Short patience has always been the enemy of long suffering.

Let's Talk: Woman to Woman

In the book of Ecclesiastes King Solomon has a kingdom like no other. He has 300 wives and 700 concubines, and not one woman was able to help him be faithful to God. A man without a faithful woman by his side is destined to lose everything God has given him. That's why I am his help meet and not the help.

What ingredient is most important to your purpose?

_____
_____
_____
_____
_____
_____
_____

How do you serve others? Explain:

_____
_____

_____
_____
_____
_____
_____

What truth has this stone given you? Explain:

_____
_____
_____
_____
_____
_____

*Am I like
a woman known
as Delilah?*

Who is Delilah? Is she here today? I believe she is like a single lady looking to get ahead at whatever price. Delilah is a woman who just happens to run into the strongest man on earth. It's probably safe to say that Sampson had demonstrated some portion of his strength before her and that demonstration may have drawn her to him. Her affiliation with Sampson made her name known among the enemies of her lover. They negotiated a deal with her to betray him. The Philistines even explained that they wanted to cause affliction upon him and she didn't care at all.

Many men today have been afflicted, incarcerated, and buried because they had a relationship with a Delilah type of woman. Proverbs 7:27 describes her this way, "Her house is the way to hell". Take a lesson from Sampson; your secrets are not safe with her. Many men and women have given away their secrets to the wrong people, including their credit, social, and strength of income. Delilah studied the art of sexual enticement. She was patient in her pursuit of his secret. Samson's purpose was to kill the Philistines and prevail through the ability that God gave him. Satan himself will pervert the gift of a woman with the tools necessary to bring him down.

She pressed him every day. In other words, she wore him out and wore him down. Some men, no matter how strong, how rich, how educated, have no defense for this weapon. Delilah is a single lady with no conscious. Her price for her services is 1100 pieces of silver from everyone involved in trapping Samson. What she is doing to Sampson is obvious, but it's like a drug and he keeps flirting with it. Sex, lies, and a sad face is what she used to get Samson's secret to make him less than the man he presently is. After three attempts she discovered the secret of his strength, she had his hair cut, collected her money, and ran. Samson was captured and the philistines put his eyes out. It's sad to say that now Samson can see what Delilah was up to.

Delilah is no amateur. Samson could not detect her plan of action. A single woman on the prowl with no discretion is a trap for dumb prey. Sampson ignorantly puts himself in the arms of the merciless and she played folly with his purpose. Will we do anything if the price is right? Can money hide our shame? Wherever Delilah went after she finished her duty she had to live with the fact that she led a judge of Israel to his death. The Philistines celebrated this day when they praised their god for delivering Samson into their hands. The Lord redeemed Samson by allowing his hair to grow again and his strength to return. Samson was placed between two pillars which the temple stood on. He pushed the pillars with all his might and the temple fell and killed about 3,000 men and women. I often wondered if Delilah was present to see what she had done. She now has beauty, praise, and money, everything a single woman would want. I wonder what the price of betrayal is these days. There is no shame today that we live a tabloid culture and no secret is safe. The televisions today are filled with many Delilah's who have no respect for the privacy of the relationship. Many women will romance a man the same way Delilah did with their intentions set on the payday ahead. What she doesn't know is that while she is waiting for her payday she is already paying the price.

Let's Talk: Woman to Woman

Women like Delilah come and go and they reap what they sow and they rarely get the chance to tell their story with joy. Delilah's betrayal cost more lives than the one she took.

What secrets have a man given you to keep?

What personal behavior do you exhibit to get what you want?

The Thin Line between God and Mate

I know it sounds like the title of an old R & B song about a man who takes a woman's tolerance of him for granted. But I chose to look at this from the pattern of women in biblical history. Many famous women in the bible had disputes and moments of frustrations with their spouse regarding the commandments of God. The events in the bible often involved married couples, so don't think that woman walked around brainless, not at all. I believed that women in the bible experienced times when their patience wore thin following her husband faith without proof.

I have debated, butted heads, and disagreed with my husband on several occasions. He's a man and I am a woman. One book says that we are from two different planets. It suggests that our ways of thinking are worlds apart but our disagreements are based on the world being a part of us. God leads us to our purpose because of our obedience to Him. There is a boundary line in my relationship between God and my mate. The bible tells me to reverence him but never over the reverence of God. He is my head under the Headship of the Lord. How do I walk this line? The thin line is based on who I am listening to. The first sin is conceived in the relationship of Adam and Eve. After listening to the serpent she wants Adam to partner with her against an ordinance of God.

The Bible teaches us not to walk as fools so that history will not repeat itself. Wake up sisters you are the thin line. Women have always had the ability to entice men to be faithful or go contrary to the will of God. In some cases in the bible she believed she was improving the situation. Let's not dismiss Adam's weakness in neglecting to restrain his wife from bringing judgment into the home. This event set the tone for relational turmoil between both sexes. It's not a matter of who is in charge, but what have you been charged to do. When Adam was put on trial by God he testified and blamed both God and the woman he gave him for his transgression. Adam allowed her to lead him across the line of restriction. I don't know the exact words Eve used to convince him or whether Adam was tempted when he saw that nothing happen when Eve ate the fruit. Whatever she did it moved him to ignore all that God said and to go full speed ahead to please his wife. Evidently, Eve had a problem with her role. She not only wanted to exceed man, but be equal to God himself. Is Eve spoiled, aggressive, rebellious, or are we like Eve. We want to be praised, we want be honored, we want to be first, we want to be adored. There is nothing wrong with wanting these things unless we are using it to challenge what you want vs. what God has said. If the Lord didn't want us to touch or eat of the fruit then why make it so deliciously tempting? On the other hand why would he make me the weaker vessel with the strongest intoxicating potion known to man? In the wrong mind it is a weapon of spiritual destruction. It's the line that I lay between God and my mate. Our female patriarchs Eve, Sarah, and Rebekah are a few who tested the line when each wanted to take charge and alter the plan which God had given to their husband.

After Eve's attempt to be equal with God, she is only mentioned two times in the Old Testament and twice in the New Testament. A prominent person in God's creation, the first woman, mother of all, is only mentioned by name four times in the whole Bible. Nothing about her death or burial is mentioned because she unlawfully put herself between God and her mate. When God specifically gives instructions to someone, any attempt to step between this covenant results in unfavorable repercussions. Eve, Sarah, and many other women found that this is a line that God has drawn for His purpose and will not move.

Remember the man is not the focus, the Lord is. The thin line is not a line to cross where you choose a side. Does the woman line of request match the line set by God? Which line does he follow? The Bible teaches us that no man can serve two masters. In the book of I Corinthians 7:34 we find the married woman in a strait betwixt two. The scriptures state that she cares for the things of this world, and how she may please her husband. It is also commanded in the book of I Thessalonians chapter 4:1-2, that she should please the Lord by faith.

It is easy for the woman to please God and her mate if they both agree. This line should not be presented as some tight wire you have to balance every day. To ensure that there is no error of choice, the things she asks of her mate should register with the will of God. Women who violate this probably already knew how to manipulate the weakness in her husband. Let's face it ladies if we want it we know how to get it. A man must be a consistent leader in order for his mate to follow and fulfill her role as a helper. Any sign in his retreat to do so provokes her self-domineering spirit to take control and make a choice that they both will be held responsible for.

In the book of Genesis chapter 16, Sarah attempts to please Abraham by fulfilling his promise with a child from Hagar, her handmaiden. Crossing this line brought many years of frustration. Her anger against Hagar kindles one day and she demands that Abraham put Hagar and the child Ishmael out of her house, because the bond woman's child would not be an heir (share the promise with her child). Abraham and Sarah argued about the mess they made and God had to referee. Even though it was Sarah's idea to use Hagar as a mid-wife, God agreed with what she said. When you lay your thin line between God and your mate make sure it's not your life line.

Let's Talk: Woman to Woman

Every man and woman will give an account of themselves to God, alone, and not as a couple. There is a thin line between God and mate, and a thinner line between the Hall of Faith and the Hall of Mistakes

Have you ever come between God and your mate?

_____
_____
_____
_____
_____
_____

Does your thin line discourage your mate?

_____
_____
_____
_____
_____
_____

What truth has this stone given you? Explain:

_____
_____

_____
_____
_____
_____
_____

Am I like a woman known as Sapphira?

Every woman should take heed in the relationship with her husband. Our marriage is meant to be a sanctuary of protection from the enemy. This covenant should bind us together in the unity of the Lord. In the Ephesians letter, Paul tells the wife to submit to our mate in everything. To some this is a hard saying, but this is a commandment with discretion and personal accountability.

In the book of Acts chapter 5, we find a woman named Sapphira who is dedicated to Ananias, her husband. She teaches us a lesson with a sad ending regarding love between God and your husband. You are allowed to love and become one flesh with him, but God says you must hate him at the same time. Your commitment and dedication to him is never a reason to break God's commandment. Every one of us shall give an account of himself to God for the deeds done in this body.

In the book of Acts chapter 5, Ananias and Sapphira teaches us that a decision of deceitfulness made in our conference together can have serious repercussions. Ananias first obligation is to love and protect his wife through God's love. He is to never put her life and relationship in danger of judgment. Ananias and Sapphira had a possession and sold it for a price. After it was sold they vowed to bring the price of the land and set it at the Apostles' feet. Ananias convinced Sapphira to keep back some of the money. The Bible says she was privy to it, which implies that Ananias spear headed the plot and she went along with it. What should Sapphira have done? She is loyal to her husband and follows his lead. They both rehearsed a lie to tell the apostles if they asked. My conversation with my husband should be pure without lies or deceit.

Sapphira did not only lie for Ananias, but against the Holy Spirit. Nothing will put us out of favor with the Lord more quickly than being a false witness. In marriage it is common for Satan to mislead and fill our hearts with temptations. Sapphira's problem is with Satan, not Ananias. My sister, Satan wants you and everything you have, including: your spouse, your children, your health, and your career. Sapphira should have wrestled with this thought "what will a man give in exchange for his soul"? The answer is nothing, not even her husband. For a selfish reason all is lost, her marriage, family, and the price she paid, which is a result of the price she kept back. Ananias lied in his actions when he laid part of the price at the Apostles feet, but Sapphira spoke the lie rehearsed by her husband. There is no comparison in the loyalty between God and your mate. She fell dead after her lie and was buried next to her husband. Where two or three are gathered together, make sure Satan is not in the midst. Your duty is to fear God, keep His commandments and keep each other in line. It is a sad thing when a husband is the cause of his wife losing her life. We don't hear about what happen after this. A home is empty, hopefully there were no children, and the money they kept was never spent by them. The next time you sit with your mate tell them that a lie can get both of us killed.

Let's Talk: Woman to Woman

Every woman is joined together to her husband by the lord, but she must not become an accessory to crime against the Lord. She should pray for immunity because the crime against the Holy Ghost carries the death penalty.

What does Sapphira teach us about lying before God?

_____
_____
_____
_____

How can Sapphira's deception hinder your purpose?

An Inner-view with Myself

No matter what purpose we are called to do we should wish the best for one another. It is a privilege to pray and ask the Lord to bless another to achieve their purpose in life. No man has seen God face to face on this time side of life. But that doesn't mean we don't stand in his presence. To stand in his presence is to stand before his Word which He speaks to us from. It is an awesome experience that we should not approach lightly with a meager respect. Let us bond by modeling a role that can ensure the spiritual excellence of our next generation.

These three things I asked the Lord to help us with every day. First help us to rise each day and fight a good fight that surrenders not to carnal desires that may evict us from the shelter of His arms. Secondly, help us build a trust with the Lord by living as a woman who can keep the faith given to us without wavering. Thirdly, Lord let us stay aware that we are running a course with hills and valleys, traps, and crossings that may discourage us from reaching our full potential.

If we want to hear the Lord say well done, we must stay focused and examine ourselves each and every day. We are given a human right to evaluate ourselves. When we are with fever, we use a thermometer to check for the degree of our illness. This is a good tool to have, but our soul is not the same. The only instrument that can examine our soul is the word of God.

This next phase introduces you to yourself. Follow the hopes, dreams, challenges, and victories of our future and past. You may find something interesting about yourself.

Remember: The woman on the cover represents the way God looks at us with no race, no face, and no respect of person.

.

Let it Grow

This segment of the book is called an inner view with myself. We may sometimes feel like a product that has been stamped "out of order". This means we are not performing at our full potential. We must take time to troubleshoot our lives from year to year and event to event to see whether we are abiding in the faith. We must be honest when we look at ourselves and seek the answer from the one who made us.

I decided to place a snapshot of questions that played a role in introducing me to myself. I pray that this approach will help recall and prepare you for a full and happy life.

My Inner-view begins:

Goal-I press toward the goal unto the prize of the high calling of God in Christ Jesus (Philippians 3:14)

(1) What is your goal for this year?

_____

_____

_____

_____

(B) _____

_____

_____

(C.)

Temptation - But every man is tempted, when he is drawn away of his own lust, and enticed. (James1:14)

(2) What is my greatest temptation?

_____

_____

_____

_____

(B)_____

_____

_____

(C.)_____

_____

_____

_____

Ministry - But be thou sober in all things, suffer hardship, do the work of an evangelist, fulfill thy ministry. (2 Timothy 4:5)

(3) What is my life ministry?

_____

_____

_____

_____

(B) _____

_____

_____

_____

(C.) _____

_____

_____

_____

Purpose - And we know that all things work together for good to them that love God, to them who are called according to his purpose. (Romans 8:28)

(4) What is my purpose?

_____

_____

_____

_____

(B) _____

_____

_____

_____

(C.) _____

_____

_____

_____

_____

Blessing- Not rendering evil for evil or railing for railing, but contrariwise blessing; knowing that ye are thereunto called, that ye should inherit a blessing. (1 Peter 3:9)

(5) Have I been a blessing to others?

_____

_____

_____

_____

(B) _____

_____

_____

_____

(C.) _____

_____

_____

_____

_____

Praise- I have trusted in thy mercy; my heart shall rejoice in thy salvation. I will sing unto the Lord, because he hath dealt bountifully with me.(Psalms 13:5-6)

(6) What is my song of praise to God?

_____

_____

_____

_____

(B) _____

_____

_____

_____

(C.) _____

_____

_____

_____

_____

Burden- Then Moses said unto the Lord, Why have you afflicted me and why have I not found favor in thy sight, that thou layest the burdens of all these people upon me (Numbers 11:11)

(7) Is my strength able to shoulder the burdens of others?

_____

_____

_____

_____

(B) _____

_____

_____

_____

(C.) _____

_____

_____

_____

Hope- It is good that a one should hope and wait quietly for the salvation of the Lord (Lamentation 3:26)

(8) What is my hope?

_____

_____

_____

_____

(B) _____

_____

_____

_____

(C.) _____

_____

_____

_____

_____

Greatest - Greater love hath no man than this; that a man lay down his life for his friends. (John 15:13)

(9) Who is my greatest love under God?

_____

_____

_____

_____

(B) _____

_____

_____

_____

(C.) _____

_____

_____

_____

Pupil - Unto Timothy, my own son in the faith, Grace, mercy, and peace, from God our Father and Jesus Christ our Lord (1Timothy 1:2)

(10) Who is my pupil?
_____
_____
_____
_____

(B) _____
_____
_____
_____

(C.) _____
_____
_____
_____

Inspirational - All scripture is given by inspiration of God, and is profitable for doctrine, for reproof, for correction, for instruction in righteousness. (II Timothy 3:16)

(11) What is my inspirational scripture when I am weak? Why?

_____

_____

_____

_____

(B) _____

_____

_____

_____

(C.) _____

_____

_____

_____

Talents - And unto one he gave five talents, to another two, and to another one; to every man according to his several ability and straightway took his journey. (Matthew 25:15)

(12) How many talents have God given me? What are they?

_____

_____

_____

_____

(B) _____

_____

_____

_____

(C.) _____

_____

_____

_____

Flaws - For I know that in me (that is, in my flesh,) dwelt no good thing, for to will is present with me, but how to perform that which is good I find not. (Romans 7:18)

(13) Do I have a flaw that hinders me?

_____

_____

_____

_____

(B)_____

_____

_____

_____

(C.)_____

_____

_____

_____

Price - Who can find a virtuous woman? For her price is far above rubies (Proverbs 31:10)

(14) What is my price?

_____

_____

_____

_____

(B) _____

_____

_____

_____

(C.) _____

_____

_____

_____

_____

Role Model - For though ye have ten thousands instructors in Christ, yet have ye not many fathers; for in Christ Jesus I have begotten you through the gospel. Wherefore I beg you be ye followers of me. (I Corinthians 4:15-16).

(15) Who is my role model?

_____

_____

_____

_____

(B)
_____

_____

_____

_____

(C.)
_____

_____

_____

Words - I fought a good fight, I have finished my course, and I have kept the faith. (II Timothy 4:7)

(16) What would be my last words to my love one?
_____
_____
_____
_____

(B) _____
_____
_____
_____

(C.) _____
_____
_____
_____

Personal Choice - And he was transfigured before them. His face did shine like the sun, and his clothes became as white as the light, and behold there appeared Moses and Elijah talking with him. (Matthew 17:2-3)

(17) If I had to speak with someone in the bible who would it be?

_____

_____

_____

_____

(B) _____

_____

_____

_____

(C.) _____

_____

_____

_____

Confidant - The heart of her husband doth safely trust in her, so that he shall have no need of spoil (Proverbs 31:11)

(18) Who is my heart safe with?

_____

_____

_____

_____

(B) _____

_____

_____

(C.) _____

_____

_____

_____

Love - But I say unto you, Love your enemies, bless them that curse you, do good to them that hate you and pray for them which despitefully use you and prosecute you. (Matthews 5:44)

(19) Which one is hard for me to do located in this scripture?

_____

_____

_____

_____

(B) _____

_____

_____

_____

(C.) _____

_____

_____

_____

Woman - Give her of the fruit of her hands and let her own works praise her in the gates (Proverbs 31:31)

(20) What do I love about being a woman?

_____

_____

_____

_____

(B) _____

_____

_____

_____

(C.) _____

_____

_____

_____

Experience- For I acknowledge my transgression: and my sin is ever before me, against thee, thee only, have I sinned and done this evil in thy sight; that thou mightiest be justified when thou speakest, and be clear when thou judgest (Psalms 51:3-4)

(21) What experience in my life would I have done differently?

_____

_____

_____

_____

(B) _____

_____

_____

_____

(C.) _____

_____

_____

_____

Memory - I will remember the works of the Lord; surely I will remember thy wonders of old. I will meditate also on all thy works and talk of thy doings (Psalms 77:11-12)

(22) What is my best memory?

_____

_____

_____

_____

(B) _____

_____

_____

_____

(C.) _____

_____

_____

_____

_____

Faith – So then faith cometh by hearing, and hearing by the word of God. (Romans 10:17)

(23) Does my faith waiver when I am in doubt?

_____

_____

_____

_____

(B) _____

_____

_____

_____

(C.) _____

_____

_____

_____

_____

Prayer- And all things, whatsoever ye shall ask in prayer, believing, ye shall receive (Matthew 21:22)

(24) What prayer has God answered for me?
_____
_____
_____
_____
_____

(B) _____
_____
_____
_____

(C.) _____
_____
_____
_____

Joy- These things have I spoken to you, that my joy may remain in you, and that your joy may be full. (John 15:11)

(25) When I am in despair, what brings me joy?

_____

_____

_____

_____

(B) _____

_____

_____

_____

(C.) _____

_____

_____

_____

_____

Character- Jesus saw Nathanael coming to him and said of him, Behold an Israelite indeed, in whom is no guile! (John 1:47)

(26) Name a character in a man that I would desire in my husband.

_____

_____

_____

_____

(B) _____

_____

_____

_____

(C.) _____

_____

_____

_____

Cry- And Peter went out, and wept bitterly (Luke 22:62)

(27) When was the last time I cried? Explain?

_____

_____

_____

_____

(B) _____

_____

_____

_____

(C.) _____

_____

_____

_____

Misconceptions- The Lord knoweth the thoughts of man, that they are vanity (Psalm 94:11)

(28) Do I have any other gods before God the Father?

_____

_____

_____

_____

(B) _____

_____

_____

(C.) _____

_____

_____

_____

Fear- Then shall they call upon me, but they shall not find me. For that they hated knowledge, and did not choose the fear of the Lord. (Proverbs 1:28-29)

(29) What is my deepest fear? Why?

_____

_____

_____

_____

(B) _____

_____

_____

_____

(C.) _____

_____

_____

_____

Patience- I waited patiently for the Lord; and he inclined unto me, and heard my cry. (Psalms 40:1)

(30) What am I patiently waiting for?
_____
_____
_____
_____
_____

(B) _____
_____
_____
_____

(C.) _____
_____
_____
_____
_____

Cease- It is an honor for a man to cease from strife, but every fool will be meddling (quarrelling). (Proverbs 20:3)

(31) What should I cease from doing?

_____

_____

_____

_____

(B) _____

_____

_____

_____

(C.) _____

_____

_____

_____

Soul- And it came to pass when he had made an end of speaking unto Saul, that the soul of Jonathan was knit with the soul of David (1 Samuel 18:1)

(32) Who is my soul knitted to? Why?

_____

_____

_____

_____

(B) _____

_____

_____

(C.) _____

_____

_____

_____

_____

Weakness- Because the foolishness of God is wiser than men; and the weakness of God is stronger than men (1 Corinthians. 1:25)

(33) In what weakness am I made stronger? Why?

_____

_____

_____

_____

(B) _____

_____

_____

_____

(C.) _____

_____

_____

_____

Actions - Talk no more exceedingly proudly; let not arrogance come out of your mouth; for the Lord is a God of knowledge, and by him actions are weighed.(1 Samuel 2:3)

(34) What actions or arrogance tried to separate me from the Love of God? How?

_____

_____

_____

_____

(B) _____

_____

_____

_____

(C.) _____

_____

_____

_____

Lessons - Not that I speak in respect of want: have I learned, in whatsoever stated I am, therewith to be content (Philippians 4:11)

(35) What is the most important lesson that I have learned?

_____

_____

_____

_____

(B)_____

_____

_____

_____

(C.)_____

_____

_____

_____

(36) Where have I been and where am I going?

(B)

(C.)

www.ingramcontent.com/pod-product-compliance
Lightning Source LLC
Chambersburg PA
CBHW060533100426
42743CB00009B/1523